Know Your Enemy Within
Bridging Knowledge and Practice of Management

Know Your Enemy Within
Bridging Knowledge and Practice of Management

It is just a bad day, not a bad life

Kooveli Madom

PARTRIDGE

Copyright © 2016 by Kooveli Madom.

| ISBN: | Softcover | 978-1-4828-7487-7 |
| | eBook | 978-1-4828-7486-0 |

Print information available on the last page.

To order additional copies of this book, contact
Partridge India
000 800 10062 62
orders.india@partridgepublishing.com

www.partridgepublishing.com/india

Contents

1

The What and Why of This Book

Disconnect between knowledge and performance or degree and delivery has been a subject of debate for long. Conclusive evidence on relevance of education for success in life and the correlation between individual professional growth and academic performance in universities are still elusive. Undisputed however are the several instances of achievers in career, business and profession who had either dropped out of college or been only mediocre in their academic performance. Equal number of cases exists where the fit between academic performance and success in profession is poor. These observations drive one to surmise that academic performance or (its surrogate) knowledge alone does not necessarily yield great results in life and *academics* is not an essential prerequisite for success.

The limited objective of this book is to demystify the role of complementary individual factors (skills, capabilities, attitudes, traits, mind-sets, need for achievement, tolerance for risk and ambiguity, preconceived notions, legacy factors, cultural context and so on) that play a great role in determining the level of achievement in whatever one pursues. *Success* only relates to goal achievement and does not stray into the area as to what goals are worth pursuing or considered laudable while measuring success. This book delves into those factors that drive individual performance beyond demonstrated knowledge and confines its discussion to the field of Management and qualifications popularly known as *MBA or its equivalents.*

The book attempts to bridge the void between knowledge of *management gained* from a formal *management* program and real world demands on practice of *management.* It exposes limitations to application of *management* concepts in isolation as well as the accelerating obsolescence of *management* theories. The intent is not to belittle value from *management* education, but to sensitise *management* students and practitioners on nurturing an open mind, on continuous learning and applying their knowledge with contextual sensitivity. The book is aimed at practising and aspiring managers, entrepreneurs and anyone, to introduce them to the practice of management and its finer nuances one encounters in day-to-day life.

Every human being is a manager irrespective of his/her social /economic status and the profession he/she is in. The simple, but not-so-obvious messages here are considered essential to practise what is learnt in formal schools, though many of these learnings would have been put to use unconsciously in our daily grind.

Our educational system fails to address critical elements essential to effectively put into practice the formal knowledge from an undergraduate /graduate program. Students of formal programs are handicapped by having no one to ask, not knowing what to ask, even feeling diffident to ask for fear of ridicule; until they are confronted with situations the like of which are illustrated here.

The syndrome of holding back genuine simple questions by students and admonishing the one raising the question by the teacher hasn't died down in our social milieu and educational system. Regressive educational system and medieval mind-set of the teaching community offer space for simple books like this, to bridge the gap between knowledge and its application. Real-life situations are visualised only when one is confronted with or when they are presented in a no-holds-barred manner; not presented as gift-wrapped knowledge in classrooms. When people try to apply knowledge from formal education innocently, gaps between the tool and its effective application surface, as surprises.

Formal education rarely address all possible variants in real-life situation for which a tool (set of tools) is expected to be applied. Formal education largely addresses theory, principles, concepts and their mechanistic application in near-ideal situations. Real-life situations are never ideal, but are open systems notorious for complexity, cacophony, unpredictability and inconsistency.

Questions such as what mix of tools to use, where, when, how, how much, how to tweak the elements, when not to use despite theory suggesting to the contrary, how to provide for situations that the theory doesn't cater for and intelligent use of knowledge, are rarely addressed.

Such gaps in our education are generally filled in by a mentor or a coach, on the job, during apprenticeship, who interprets situations for the intern, in the context of the theory. He also extends the comfort and confidence to carve a judicious just-in-time amalgam of concepts, apply them, interpret the outcome and continuously tweak to arrive at desired results.

This free-wheeling dialogue is what this book attempts to achieve, to give the reader a sense of what to expect and how to handle the same. The role of this book essentially is to be a coach or mentor; not a lecturer on theory. This is not a replacement for text books. Instead, it serves the purpose of supplementary or a value added reading for someone excited about the topic. I hope inquisitive readers will find some value, help supplement the content and educate the author by sharing their own experiences and views.

The book chronicles evolution of management theories, touches upon the transitions in management concepts over time, contrarian views on some of the much celebrated management theories and models, management as an open system and the significance of soft elements of management (organisation and individual levels) as much as the hard elements. It addresses the issue of employability of graduates, complimentary traits expected of MBAs that are fundamental prerequisites for managers and built into entry requirements for some MBA programs

A compendium of drivers of success and failure in goal attainment, the book attempts to expose what are not taught in MBA classrooms: individual thought processes guiding actions and never discussed, but intrinsic and practised. Thought processes make people who they are. The book is a distilled essence of situational experiences, observation, analysis, learnings from consulting practice, the HR community and management students. I trust the reader will be able to connect with me.

This is not a nineteen actionable tips to earn one billion dollars in hundred days for any ordinary person. There are no short cuts and smart tips to achievement; only hard conscientious effort. The author believes it is more enduring to educate one to fish than make promises of giving it free.

The book aims to open the reader's mind to unravel the self, others and the environment around, to come up with own ways to achieve one's goal. Strategies to goal achievement vary across individuals, each devising methods in harmony with the self and contextual factors. There is no one right approach, there could be many. The intent is to expose the possibilities and the mental blocks we carry in decisively choosing a path, that impede our progress. Self-awareness helps overcome self- inflicted roadblocks to reach our goal.

Some of the content may sound hilarious and radical; bordering on perceived illegality, less than ethical, intrigue, aggressive, and challenging practices masked as espoused idealism. Such an approach is a deliberate attempt to expose the reader to realities, guiding one into actions considered necessary. This potentially controversial approach is attributed to hard learning from experience: what they don't teach in Harvard but essential to apply what is learnt in Harvard.

Business schools dwell on solutions with a caveat: everything else remaining constant. Real world elements are never constant. They also exert considerable influence over everything around, multiplying the complexity. The earth doesn't stop turning around its axis for someone to execute a meticulously carved business plan.

The intent is not to ridicule formal education or radicalise minds, but bring to surface the turbulence we encounter every day and significance of the mind behind the matter, in handling the shocks and surprises. The word 'he' wherever it appears in the text refers to both genders without orientation to any one gender.

This book has gained from handling several assignments for MBA students from universities across the globe the author has undertaken, about three decades of management consulting practice, association with management education, management students, employers and those employed. Experience from the author's own life is not the least of what has contributed to it.

Reflections into the past, experiences of failure and successes, interactions with diverse individuals: achievers and otherwise, observations of traits of apparently ordinary people venturing and finding their space, contributed immensely to this book. Success stories in the technology space, emerging entrepreneurship by the just-out-of-college types, stories of rags to riches* and otherwise of unsuccessful

---

* A run-away table boy in a tea shop rising to a star hotel chain owner in two decades, a low level office assistant rising to own the most sought after chain of schools and their franchisees in the IT capital, a once small time electronic components trader running the largest mobile services company, second generation of a fuel dispenser in a gas station running the largest business empire and becoming the richest man in the country, an ordinary school teacher's son and his small team creating benchmarks in the technology services industry, a high school car washer boy completing his engineering degree and employed as a senior engineer in an MNC and also managing other own business individuals from highly educated class, influenced the content and contour of this book. These stories reinforce the fact that, the mind plays a more significant role in determining who we are and where we reach, than formal knowledge acquisition.

We have witnessed highly accomplished people driven from their state of holistic comfort to one of drudgery, due to extreme disconnect between their illusions and the ways of the real world. They live in a world of their own making with an artificial shell around them, to seek comfort and avoid interaction with the real world with its variety, uncertainty and imperfections. The belief that retreating into a shell will relieve the individual of the effort to understand, and the need for developing coping mechanisms to deal with the real world, are, at best, illusions. Withdrawal is never a solution to a problem. It helps in denial and, at best, a short-term relief, but not a solution. A solution is found only when we take the bull by the horns and handle the problem as a challenge, not as a nuisance that vanishes if we deny its existence. Some primitive communities with low worldly exposure carry the notion that not discussing an issue will make it disappear

This booklet is an attempt to recognise this enemy within us, examine what made people turn out to be who they became, and draw possible lessons on worldly wisdom for goal achievement. Since most of these learnings are experiential, it is quixotic to expect the green horns to have mastered these real life lessons to be effective practically, despite their high academic credentials. This booklet is a small beginning in sharing experiences, pre-empting reinventing the wheel, building confidence and reducing the learning curve. It is believed such open sharing of experience could relieve the learner of the discomfort of exposure, fear of exposing his ignorance or having to seek advice on embarrassing situations.

There is near unanimity in the perception that, a void exists between what is taught and learnt and what one experiences in the practice of management. A fresher realises the swings between what he has learnt and the practices he is confronted with in real organisations. The tools and tricks he has learnt do not seem to work the way he has been made to believe. This book tries to expose some of these anomalies, with the intent to introduce the reader to this void. It alerts the reader to be on guard while using the tools and techniques, the need to carry a fresh mind, not to take theories as absolute truth and true for ever. Most theories get revisited, challenged or rewritten as fresh concepts, fresh considerations emerge and new practices evolve. The practitioner needs to be alert, to challenge his own understanding.

One has to find one's own trajectory to one's intended destination. One has to listen to one's mind, discover own path and accept the onus for the outcome. The adage is 'follow your heart and find your space, you are more capable than what you believe you are'.

Driven by compulsions turning into opportunities for learning and the brazen courage to question popular wisdom, the objective is to share the experience, in order that it may be of value to others, avoid same mistakes, can anticipate and be prepared to handle situations better. It is about what one could expect while traversing this path, how one could handle the turbulence and discover your real you. There is no one right trajectory to success. The choice depends on contextual factors, emotional traits of the individual traversing the path and competence to steer through.

2

Motivation for This Book

Reflecting on the chequered past under single parent childhood makes one feel blessed; an inappropriate statement in our social context. Torrent of hurdles drove one into spurts of stifled rebellious thoughts, amid persistent reminders of being cursed, helpless, inferior and worthless. Innocent optimism becomes the lone driving force to pursue secret goals. Not knowing how to evaluate opportunities, the value of what is in hand or how to reach the distant visible goal-post; one reconciles to accept what came by chance and native intelligence: many missed opportunities when juxtaposed against the present context and possibilities.

The logical option under duress is to take the path of least resistance, accepting the outcome as destiny. The difficult task is to closely guard and nurture the innocent belief that one can, it is possible and will make it. This belief becomes the last straw of optimism to move forward. Is it this belief that makes it a reality, in the absence of external props? One can speculate the outcome depending on who is in the debate, what school of thought one believes in and ones' prior experience.

Moving against the tide is a challenge as well as a source of confidence and inspiration from strands of rewards on the horizon. Challenges are catalysts for confidence-building from discovery and self-learning from setbacks, to handle surprises. Overcoming distractions and experience of resisting detractors, enhances belief in oneself. Compulsions to move forward guided by own rules, turn out to be blessings in disguise. Not many will have the opportunity to tread own path and experiment, early in life. Is it an opportunity for self-discovery and learning or a curse impeding one's growth?

Formal education is a privilege to membership in exclusive clubs and a license to challenge conventional wisdom, that otherwise would be typecast as manifestation of ignorance. Management education is a privileged club membership. Club membership is an enabling factor, provides access to resources, those who matter and elite circles, but doesn't directly translate into achievement.

One has to learn the art of reaching one's goal, ingeniously, using tools from formal education or even challenging them. Same tool used differently by equally competent persons turns out different outcomes. Equally endowed persons may follow different trajectories for the same *origin destination set,* ending up with different outcomes. Both could be successful depending on what one considers to be success; and when and how success is measured.

Motivation for this book is the visibility gained into both sides of the fence, the misery and the glory, and having struck a deal marrying the two. Sharing of this experience may help demystify and partially eliminate the discomfort for someone going through turbulent times.

3

Why a Negative Caption

Human tendency is to look outside the window to point a finger at, for our problems or predicament. Driving theme of this book is that, most of our problems are largely our own making, our inability to foresee, our incompetence to handle issues effectively, greed for results without efforts or a combination of these. Compounding this, are our own contribution to the making of the problem in the form of preconceived notions, emotional weakness, our view of the world around us, knowledge of the self and others. Self-inflicted hurdles hold us back from appropriate timely action or catalyse counterproductive behaviour such as short cuts or ineffective measures. Denial, impatience, greed, mental blocks and other affective traits adversely affect the vigour with which we act on issues and retard our progress. In essence, we are our own enemy by our thought processes and actions. If we look within and recognise this, we will be better placed to handle our problems.

Dictionary meaning of the word 'enemy' ranges from a foe, an adversary, an opponent, a rival, a nemesis, an antagonist, a combatant, a challenger, a hostile party; all pointing to externally focused destructive elements. The message from this book is that the enemy is not external but well within us and manageable, if we want to. If it is manageable, then why are we not managing it, in a manner beneficial to us? The answer to this question needs understanding of the self. What is it within us, that turns out to be inimical to us, holding back timely appropriate action? How we can control it and why we are not doing so? The word 'enemy' is used to mean: a catalyst for self-destruction through inability to act in a purposive manner, due to own inhibitions, apprehensions, mind-sets and perceptions about the self, others and the world around.

In its practical sense, an enemy is anything that impedes progress towards our stated or intended objectives. An enemy need not be tangible, obtrusive or external but can be invisible, subtle, within and creeping. Enemy's actions to obstruct progress need not be physical, visible, violent, external or discrete. It can be unobtrusive, subconscious, working on our psyche and invisible. Examples include disinterest, illusions of fear or complacency within, in acting decisively as needed towards goal attainment. This is in contrast to our tendency to look outward for reasons for failure or our unfortunate predicament.

We have to recognise that we ourselves are responsible for our problems as much as the external forces and internal factors are more potent to retard progress than external impediments. Our external orientation to our problems is because of our poor visibility into our self, denial to recognise presence of negative elements within us and reluctance to act on it. It calls for introspection, humility and maturity to look within. If we have the mind to look within, we will be surprised with the innumerable possibilities of effectively handling it at no cost. The negative caption reinforces the significance of internal factors determining who we are, what we are, why we are and where we reach.

4

Mind and Management

Human mind is a complex machine to define, decipher and control. Despite advances in technology and knowledge, understanding the human mind, how it behaves and how to guide / control it, is still a little known territory. Psychometric tests are the best available tools to judge human personality and predict behaviour in diverse situations. Outcome of these tests is at best indicators of likely behaviour of an individual in similar contexts. They are not deterministic and therefore of limited predictive value in specific cases. Human behaviour is guided by several factors working together and influencing each other. These influences are contextual, additive and multiplicative (field theory) and determine the course of action one chooses to take.

Mind is the critical element determining where one goes and what one does, more than the brain that logically processes data. While the brain is part of the visible, tangible world of the body; mind is the invisible, transcendent world of thought, feeling, attitude, belief and imagination. The mind is the manifestations of thought, perception, emotion, determination, memory and imagination that take place within the brain. Mind refers to the thought processes of reason (Controlmind).

Mind plays a significant role in determining what one chooses to do, what factors guide the choice, how one does it and the act of doing it. Success or otherwise is determined by thought processes in the mind, the way these are processed and decisions the mind takes to act upon them.

There is no single agreed upon definition of the mind. Dr. Daniel Siegel coined the term "mindsight" to describe the human capacity to perceive the mind of the self and others. According to him, mind is a powerful lens, through which we can understand our inner lives with more clarity, integrate the brain, and enhance our relationships with others. Mindsight is a kind of focused attention that allows us to see the internal workings of our own minds. It lets us "name and tame" the emotions we are experiencing, rather than being overwhelmed by them. An integral part of the mind comprises the relational process of energy and information flowing between and among people. Our minds are created within relationships - including the one that we have with ourselves.

Each of us has a unique mind: unique thoughts, feelings, perceptions, memories, beliefs and attitudes and a unique set of regulatory patterns. These patterns shape the flow of energy and information inside us and we share them with other minds (Brainpages). The Mind refers to a person's understanding of things, his conscience and thought process (Mindbrain). The human mind is a key driver of one's success in whatever one endeavours in.

5

Bane of Collectivism

CONFORMIST SOCIETIES

The practice of management is context driven. There is no FAQ (Frequently Asked Questions) one can refer to find quick book solutions to all management problems.

Indian (*eastern*) society believes in *collectivism* as against *individualism* of the *west*. *Collectivism* expects conformity; a behavioural trait that is restrictive; eulogised as team work, participative and democratic. Conformity robs the individual of the freedom to think and act independently, and chart own strategies to reach ones' goal. Collectivism reduces freedom to *freedom within bounds*. It turns out to be a compulsion to fall in line with the thought leader or the powerful. Collectivism is practising double standards: what is good for the follower is not good for the preacher. It is regressive and frustrating to be compelled to be in conformist circles.

Collectivism feeds hypocrisy, driving victims to invent circuitous paths to achieve their closely held goal. This is the experience in collective societies practising a convenient form of socialism. Practice of collectivism is a drain on societies' intellectual energy, spent on managing internal strife. This is a clear manifestation of the *enemy within*, driven by externalities and demanding coping mechanisms to manage these externalities.

Collectivism drives suboptimum realisation of individual potential, driven by a game of one-up-man-ship; the syndrome of first among equals. Strategies to work around *collectivist approach* are less spoken about, but quietly understood and unobtrusively acted upon by enterprising individuals, to buy peace and achieve one's ends. Some of the frequently used terms to refer to this syndrome are connections, networks, contacts, service providers, outsourcing and so on.

Ingenuity and guts play a major role in choosing the unspoken path to one's ends. Collectivism, in essence, is a tool to legitimise and preserve the pecking order / veiled authority of the powerful. Collectivism is ingenious social engineering!

Collectivism and its consequence, conformism, tend to typecast individuals. It makes it difficult for individuals to rediscover and carry an image different from what they have been seen as in the past (legacy image). This is a hurdle for individuals and societies to progress and to break from the past. Managing other's expectation of the self and to express individuality become a drain on one's energy and drag on enterprise. Collective societies tend to be like crabs in a bottle, not letting anyone get out when everyone wants to. Unfortunately no one wants to speak about it, under the illusion that everyone wants to be in when no one wants to be in, if only they had a choice to do so, without anyone knowing about it; flagrant hypocrisy.

The transition phase of ejecting out of a conformist group (shifting orbits) is painful and risky, as the outcome of the effort is unknown and uncertain. To exercise individualism, one has to eject out of his *present* (micro society) and embrace a new identity, preferably in an alien society, devoid of the hangover of legacy. The *most individualistic* societies are made up of immigrants. Immigrants with no baggage of legacy, start afresh with a new identity (or no identity) and freedom from *expectations*. That probably is the reason why the United States (a country of immigrants) is the most individualistic society; its identity is one of materialism embraced by individuals, despite a diverse past, in their own motherland.

In collective societies, the individual is a product (victim) of inherited circumstances, that turns out to be an impediment to realise his true potential. He is seen through the coloured glass of his legacy or background. Circumstances include birth (parentage and place), formative years, childhood experiences, education, the company he keeps out of choice or compulsion, exposure or lack of it, emotional support or lack of it, social status, connections, access to resources and freedom to act sans constraints / compromise.

In collective societies, individuals may choose to embrace compromising situations in the short term for long term benefits: the strategy of *losing a battle to win a war*. Enterprising individuals recognise this small price for a potential gain and manoeuvre this path deftly, without remorse. In some communities, even attempts to express one's individuality (if it goes against group norms), are considered as attempts to break away, triggering potential ostracism, social rejection and subtle non-cooperation.

One has to battle several odds just to be what one wants to be. To endure such social isolation, one needs high motivation, tenacity, clarity of purpose, self-awareness and the will to cleverly orchestrate (manipulate) other's expectations to realise own goals. These constraints drive the *initiated* to flee their shackled close community for greener pastures, without the baggage of legacy. Green pastures could be an alien land: from villages to towns/cities/foreign soil, unconstrained by proximity to immediate groups / *significant others* with divergent expectations.

In closed groups, with limited opportunity to experiment and explore, immediate group members become the *significant others*, who exercise emotional control over group members. Those from rural areas are *de facto* held captive by their immediate circles, making it difficult to break out and pursue opportunities outside, despite their inherent capabilities. Those bred in large diverse communities (metros, cities) are relatively free of such constraints of emotional bonding. This is the reason why some parents send their children to far flung locations to shield from the influence of immediate groups, develop a wider perspective and the capacity to break out and stand out.

Many youngsters become victims of their inability to manage others' expectations of them and influence of their *significant others* on their growth. This reminds us of the adage *you are known by the company you keep.* One tends to get typecast based on one's immediate circles, as immediate circles have a great influence on the individual and shape what one can accomplish. It is a challenge to be inside and enjoy the real autonomy of the world outside. It needs a strong supporting environment and emotional strength, to withstand pressures of insiders to conform and to be faithful followers; against the desire to experience true freedom. The import of these factors and the coping mechanisms needed can be appreciated only from the experience of going through such situations. The art or science of managing emotional issues cannot be ingrained through lecture sessions: reason why advanced management programs have elements of experiential learning to near-mimic real-life situations.

Collectivism is a mask to impose individualism of the powerful / the select few, over the masses, robbing the masses of their individualism. This is what happens in institutions that are outwardly known as *democratic* but are essentially feudalistic. A truly democratic institution will end up in anarchy. Even democratic institutions are guided by the dictates of a few, but stage managed as democratic. Recall the role of a *chief whip* in a parliamentary system to ensure that freedom is exercised as dictated by the boss (leader).

CONFORMISM IN FAMILIES

Conformism exists even in families where some are more equal than others: elders, male members or even those privileged to hold that position from proximity or special affection to the *head*. Conformist societies and their microcosm (families) coerce the individual through emotional blackmail to follow the *majority,* devoid of transparent logic or merit. In essence, these are subtle tools to perpetuate the agenda of the *invisible* powers. Eastern culture is marked by subtle coercive tactics to conform. Inexperience makes one oblivious to what is brewing behind well-sounding advice from good Samaritans. Reflections on the past reveal how one was led through a path of roses into a potential grave, presented as paradise.

FREEDOM

Freedom is the most valued intangible commodity. Freedom makes one responsible, but giving it out is feared by the one withholding it. *Empowerment* makes the empowered accountable, responsible, motivated and productive and enhances self-esteem. Freedom is withheld by those who fear losing control over others and the privileges associated with control. Empowerment is exploited (misinterpreted) as hidden opportunities for rent seeking sans accountability. This syndrome is more conspicuous in public organisations where *power* is a synonym for privilege without accountability.

Enterprising individuals should extract their freedom to experience the sense of liberation and give expression to their entrepreneurship; not for rent seeking. Easily said than practised! It needs all the tricks (not available for ordering from a menu card) of ingenuity, to extract autonomy and liberate oneself from the clutches of legitimate / illegitimate authority. Freedom is not *given* but *taken* using subtle means. Once you are known to extract freedom, it starts flowing naturally, as you earn membership in elite clubs of those who have managed their freedom. One need not be an MBA to know how to extract ones' freedom. One learns from life's experience along the way.

6

Individual Traits and Contextual Diversity

SWEET TALKERS AND STRAIGHT TALKERS

Sweet (or smooth) talkers take one through a rose garden to be dumped on a bed of thorns. Straight talkers mean what they speak, speak what they mean and deliver what is promised. Sweet talkers are pleasant to deal with, not worthy of keeping company; straight talkers cause temporal discomfort, but tend to be reliable, enduring and remembered for good reasons. How does one identify a sweet talker in the first instance and how does one guard oneself from being a victim of sweet talks? It just has to be experienced. A once victim of sweet talks can easily smell the rat and separate the two with ease.

HONESTY

Though unpleasant and expensive in some societies, honesty and integrity get rewarded over time, at a short term price. Long term rewards are satisfying while short term achievements get one status, name, fame and temporal bargaining power. In our enthusiasm to achieve our goals, and our need for social status and affiliation, we tend to trade long term interests for short term comforts. One soon realises the consequences, may stay on or change track, depending on ones' needs and the price one is willing to pay for it.

FEAR

Fear is the worst enemy to progress. Listen to your heart (mind) and use your brain. The heart drives the engine of action. The brain is a tool, to be used judiciously. Overuse / misuse / abuse / underuse of brain are detrimental. A weak heart that confronts with the logical brain is debilitating and a recipe for disaster. Avoid being a victim of analysis leading to paralysis, as outcome of analysis is only probabilistic; of little predictive value in specific cases. Domain of analysis is confined to the past or the present, but decisions are for the future. One has to emotionally train oneself to deal with surprises (risk), characteristic of probabilistic outcomes. *Fear of failure* and *need for achievement* are two ends of a spectrum. One has to tread cautiously to strike a balance, considering one's goals and the price one is willing to pay for them

SUCCESS

Success is largely driven by the affective elements in each one of us; the cognitive elements playing only an analytical role. This explains the paradox: some educated people not being successful and some ordinary ones rising from nowhere to become icons. Ability to effectively use emotional elements, to maximise return from cognitive analysis, is an asset to be acquired through practice and difficult to measure. These traits fall under popular terms such as intuition, emotional / social intelligence, emotional maturity, worldly wisdom, entrepreneurship, *et al.*

STRIKING A BALANCE

One has to strike a balance between the need for achievement and the fear of failure, as well as pursue a fine balance between caution and courage, that are context driven. No classroom session can tutor one on what line of thinking and action one should adopt in every situation. Broad guidelines mean little, when situational dynamics cannot be visualised at a granular level. Guidelines in isolation are not operational; they have only academic and statistical value.

7

Factors Influencing Our Predicament

AWARENESS

Strategies adopted for obstructing progress of other's goal achievement are wide ranging in terms of their nature, visibility, tenure, severity, longevity and impact on the target. Impact could be creating physical barriers; impeding or making expensive access to resources essential to achieve goal, creating fissures to weaken valuable networks, surreptitiously planting and abetting insiders to do the job and - most important - playing on the victim's psyche to create an invisible self-inflicted barrier to progress.

Existence of an *enemy within* is tantamount to kicking a self-goal. Chanakyas of the modern era excel in the art of intrigue, to destroy their business / political nemesis, and abet and celebrate self-goals by their opponents. The art of intrigue can stoop down to targeting individual rivals / competitors within organisations, professional / business rivals and more. What applies to states, kingdoms and organisations are true at individual levels in a diluted / improvised version. Young professionals need to be conscious of potential adventurism by visible and invisible rivals, by being in a state of readiness to face such situations; that rarely call for any direct action. Awareness and readiness to act are the defence against any misadventure of detractors; akin to a nuclear deterrent to keep the potential enemy at bay. A deterrent is most effective when not used. The objective is to be on guard to pre-empt a situation that may call for its use.

FREEDOM TO ACT

Freedom is a state of our mind. Freedom has to be believed to exist and experienced. A visibly independent person may not experience freedom to act due to frivolous, non-existent, extraneous considerations adversely affecting his ability to act decisively. These could include imaginary fears of how the *significant others* will perceive his action, potential criticism, adverse comments, loss of goodwill or the image of a nice guy, potential collateral damage and so on. Over-brooding to please others, robs one of his freedom, jeopardising own interests.

What make some people succeed against odds, while others buckle from own mind-sets, are the mental blocks on the *rights* and *wrongs*, fear of the unknown and the imaginary consequences of being seen as different. Lack of initiative due to low *need for achievement*, misplaced notions about how one's *significant others* will likely perceive their action, fear of bold expression or action that may be out of sync with close social circles or significant others, are significant elements of the *enemy within*. The emotional blocks reflect deficit of true independence in thinking and decisive action, stifled by subconscious debilitating external dependence. Inability to exercise freedom amounts to being subjected to effective emotional blackmail by detractors: imaginary or real and external to achieve their own ends.

Any action or inaction irrespective of its intent or nature will be subject to criticism / comments by someone. One need not bend backwards to please or carry all and anyone with him, if that jeopardises own interest. One should steadfastly guard the hierarchy of own interests to remain focused and effective. Clarity of purpose, determination and decisiveness mark effective individuals; not necessarily making everyone happy and buying peace from all quarters. Below is a quote from a spiritual Guru Sri Sri Ravi Shankar:

"A plum once said, 'just because a banana lover came by, I converted myself into a banana. Unfortunately, his taste changed after a few months and so I became an orange. When he said I was bitter I became an apple, but he went in search of grapes. Yielding to the opinions of so many people, I have changed so many times that I no more know who I am. How I wish I had remained a plum and waited for a plum lover.'

Just because a group of people do not accept you as you are, there is no necessity for you to strip yourself of your originality. You need to think good of yourself, for the world takes you at your own estimate. Never stoop down or bend backwards in order to gain quick recognition. Never let go of your true self to win a relationship. In the long run, you will regret that you traded your greatest assets – your uniqueness, for momentary validation. Even Gandhi was not accepted by many people. The group that does not accept you as YOU is not Your world.

There is a world for each one of you, where you shall reign as king /queen by just being yourself. Find that world… In fact, that world will find You.

What water can do, gasoline cannot and what copper can, gold cannot. The fragility of the ant enables it to move and the rigidity of the tree enables it to stay rooted. Everything and everybody has been designed with a proportion of uniqueness to serve a purpose that we can fulfil only by being our unique self. You as you alone can serve your purpose and I as I alone can serve my purpose. You are here to be you… Just YOU.

There was a time in this world when a Krishna was required and he was sent; A time when a Christ was required and he was sent; a time when a Mahatma was required and he was sent; There came a time when you were required on this planet and hence you were sent. Let us be the best we can be.

In the history of the universe, there has been nobody like you and to the infinity of time to come, there will be no one like you. Existence should have loved you so much that it broke the mould after making you, so that another of your kind will never get repeated.

RESPONSE TO SITUATIONS

Perception that response to any trigger: situation, action, provocation or communication has to be of the same kind, is misplaced. Many times ignoring the trigger (in terms of obtrusive response) may turn out to be the most intelligent action, born out of wisdom. Silence is also a response, if the meaning of silence is understood by the one asking for the response. The meaning of silence has to be understood depending on from where it originates and in what context. Each person sends out different (unique) messages through obtrusive inaction (silence). When wisdom prevails over knowledge, it may result in silence (no response or inaction) as a response. Many trying situations will naturally find a solution if it is given the benefit of time. It needs maturity to draw meaning from silence and courage to choose the path of silence.

8

Is Obedience to Your Boss ('Yes Sir') Always the Right Way?

Many times young professionals are confronted with the question 'should I always agree or should I differ with my boss' in their initial years of working life. What happens if I differ? Will I lose my job? My promotion? My increment? Get a poor appraisal rating? Get into the bad books of the boss? Be red flagged? My competitor (colleague) will overtake me? I may lose opportunities for progression?

Unfortunately, they have no one to ask this question. Not even their educated parents, who may not understand the undercurrents in the organisational milieu and their ward's context in the work place. Only he/she has to take a call based on his/her own best judgment and personality traits.

Why personality traits? Every person is designed differently, has his/her unique approach to situations, despite commonalities of education, family, social and economic background. No one is right or wrong in an absolute sense. Everyone is right in his own way. It is not advisable to mimic your colleague only because you found him manage an additional rise or a recommendation from the boss the previous year or the last quarter. It always pays in the long run to be yourself. Do not draw conclusions from your colleague's achievement in isolation in one year or quarter. A deeper examination may tell you that you just don't want to be like him, even if that cost you your job! This (your colleague's stocks rocking!) could also be due to an unholy nexus between your colleague and your common boss, and the boss rewarding him for his collusion in an unholy act or for a unique chemistry between the two. Such opportunities are unlikely to be repeated and following that path amounts to, you losing your identity and even denying yourself more valuable rewards.

The above scenario (your colleague over you) and much more are possible. Not necessarily each time your dissent goes against you. Boss being who he is and how he has become a boss, is intelligent enough to separate the wheat from the chaff. And not every boss is the same. There may be bosses who have become who they are, through means that may not be broadcast. Benefiting from the magnanimity of such bosses is not worth. Such opportunities have short life. Such bosses became self-styled heroes due to contextual factors / compulsions: unemployment, poverty, license raj, sycophancy, favouritism, nepotism and so on, in an insulated economy. Fear of losing / denial overshadowed all logic. No longer true now. So come out of the shell, express and experience yourself.

We are now part of an interconnected global village where competition, competence, openness, integration, cross-border movement of men, materials, ideas, capital, labour and information constitute the rule, and are not a choice. In a competitive market, it is only your competence and the value you bring to the organisation you are in / your client, that works. It doesn't matter who you are, your age, colour of your skin, gender, origin, looks, parentage and so on, if you have the stuff and deliver, your approach and argument is logical, you demonstrate your capabilities (not selfies, posturing, foul-mouthing colleagues, carrying work place stories) and prove your worth. Your employer / customer (your employer is a customer to you) are watching if you can deliver value.

We are in an era of near-perfect competition in the global space; not even hyperlocal monopolies, except in a few businesses with micro-market characteristics such as real estate that cannot be transported / replicated across geographies. The internet is a great leveller and symbolises near-perfect competition and equality of opportunity. An individual can take on a multi-national! Small time gimmicks of yester years: contacts, recommendation, religious, linguistic, regional affiliation and such considerations rarely yield value.

The author is personally baffled by the experience (several occasions, different bosses, different kinds of organisations) of speaking his mind, unmindful of how it will be taken. In most cases, being a contrarian has only returned pleasant surprise for being candid, despite the availability of easy path of agreeing with the boss and losing nothing, except not getting noticed! You even earn a distinct identity, a brand, to your advantage by being candid.

In employment interviews, it is expected that candidates participate in the dialogue and not limit himself to yes / no responses. The interviewer is trying to unravel your social intelligence and communication skills, which is only possible if you engage in a conversation, demonstrating your articulating skills, in situations where you may have to differ. You need not always think the same as the interviewer and it is not expected. This may sound strange when juxtaposed against tips one gets in interviewing coaching sessions offered by some training institutes.

You don't get targeted for being honest if you have a logic for being different, you articulate your case convincingly, speak from your heart, not be hypocritical, do not carry a hidden agenda, demonstrate your knowledge on the topic of difference, show mutual respect, you are consistent and you hold your ground (test of your conviction to be a contrarian - are you doing so for cheap popularity to stand out?).

In some meetings, participants tend to sing in chorus 'I agree' whenever the boss comes up with a proposal or a solution to a problem for discussion, and ask for feedback or comments from the participants. Participants believe that the boss is looking for *yes men* (or women) to endorse his line of thinking. He doesn't need it. He is the boss and is entitled to take his own decisions. He is not in a vote counting / popularity enhancement mission to get his idea passed.

The boss is looking for ideas from participants different from his own, to add value, to come up with a different / better solution, bring new perspectives, forewarn him on potential collateral negatives, point out lapses and so on. The Indian / eastern (*yours obediently*) mind-set has been to always to agree with the boss, teacher, parent and any elder (Cultural dimensions of management).

It is not a crime to differ with another, whoever that be. What is needed is, to have a convincing reason for differing and being able to articulate the same. In the western culture passivity, inability to add value by contributing to ideas is flagged as incompetence. Next time you are in a meeting or someone asks for your views/ comments, spend quality time on the subject, apply your mind, do some research if needed, give your well-articulated and considered inputs to add real value. You are paid to add value in any and many ways, not just be a passive decorative piece in the office. No employer can afford to keep paid wax models in glass cages.

9

MBA to Manager
The Transition Dilemma

MBA programs and the curriculum presuppose capitalistic / free market economy of the west as the operating environment for businesses. The entire theory on management is based on the assumption of operating in a free market competitive environment and player's objective is to maximise private gains. But many economies are not operating in a free market environment. For instance, India is an emerging transitional economy with imperfections of a free market. Theories evolved for a free market many times are not applicable to work in a non-free market economy. It is expected that MBAs apply their business management knowledge with care, diligence and application of mind when working in environments that are distortions of a free market. Examples of misplaced over adventurous use of knowledge in a narrow sense with disastrous consequences include global investment meltdown, Lehman Brothers collapse, sub-prime crisis and so on. The key word to reflect maturity in a manager is *application orientation and contextual sensitivity.* Such an approach calls for conditions as cited in the chart below.

Conditions ensuring Application Orientation and Contextual Sensitivity among Manager*s*

(a) Incisive analysis to know the why of the what from observation of current and emerging happenings.

(b) You to be critical and not lean towards mechanical conformity.

(c) Knowing limitations of any approach, before flaunting on its benefits.

(d) Recognising knowledge is only a tool, a framework and not a solution by itself.

(e) Developing ability to see the invisible, example: role of lending, derivatives and investment advisors.

(f) Recognising the multidisciplinary character and the need to distil problem from symptoms, know what to apply, how, when, where, at what rate, by whom.

It is essential to realise that organizations are not designed on lines of functional specialties in the MBA program syllabi, for mechanical application of theory. You need to mentally model the problem using the frameworks to apply the functional knowledge judiciously. Real organizations operate in a dynamic real world. They are not carved out for application of theory. It is essential to analyse and understand, to intelligently decide on the tools, techniques and knowledge to apply unobtrusively. Recognise that an MBA is not a passport to success / recognition. An MBA may give you the benefit of doubt and help entry, but to stay there you have to prove yourself. The benefit of doubt shifts the onus on to you, with high expectations. The initial benefit of doubt as well as the privileges / edge over others will sustain only if you exceed expectations.

(g) Being open to exposure to pitfalls, wrong application, learn from mistakes and analysis of events: ex. Enron, Failure cases of ERP.

(h) You to be sensitive to the dynamic nature of complex influencing factors.

(i) You have to focus on timely and quality delivery.

Realise that capability is not rewarded. What is rewarded is demonstration in holistic problem solving and contribution to value creations.

(j) You realising that organisations work in teams, you have to learn to enjoy team work, respect others and be able to command respect by your conduct and contribution. You have to inculcate team work, collaboration and continuous learning.

(k) You realising' in real world, no data is given / will come to you. You have to get / create data which may not be complete/relevant/ accurate/ perfect to meet your requirements. The difficult job is what data to get and how to get it, and making it happen. Getting relevant, reliable and current data is a challenge.

Organizations spend enormous senior executive time / resources to gain access to quality reliable accurate current data. Data is not numbers in table / excel form ready for analysis, but include informal data gathered from informal sources and situations, observations, third party sources, surrogates, perceptions and best judgment. Formal reports are not necessarily the best source of useful information.

(l) Management is not mathematics or deterministic.

Management decisions, inferences, strategies and actions are based on most probable outcomes expected from available information and judgment, in an open and dynamic environment. Intolerance to ambiguity is a major hurdle.

(m) Successful managers are not necessarily MBAs (successful college dropouts).

(n) You realising that

- People don't behave on theoretical lines of behavioural sciences, as other things are never constant.
- Knowledge alone doesn't guarantee result. Knowledge, Attitudes, Practices, Actions collectively lead to results.
- Importance of emotional maturity, judgment, attitudes, determination, perseverance, focus is to be recognised.
- It is easy to acquire knowledge resources, but not people with the right bend of mind to generate outcomes.
- Passion, grit, confidence, killer instinct, persistence and risk taking lead to success. Some of these attributes are to be acquired and practiced.
- Success once does not guarantee success next time, it has to be worked towards every time afresh.
- In organisational life there are no pass marks. It has to be 100% all times, as clients and customers don't accept nor can you sell anything less than the best, as you are charging them for 100% for best in class products / services.

- There is no level playing field (as clamoured for by industry associations). You need to take advantage of the uneven terrain and compete in the turbulence (Hamel and Prahlad). Competitive advantages are many times contextual and unique to individuals and organizations.
- Politicians generate competitive advantages for themselves by strategizing for long term.

  You will never know the true intent, which is always a hidden agenda. What appears innocuous would have been the result of deep rooted thinking, analysis, strategies and plans. They completely change the established rules of the game, as politics is the game of possibilities.

- External environmental management is equally or more important than intra organisational management.
- At lower levels technical skills are important, at middle levels technical and people skills and at the top levels it is strategy and environmental management capabilities that matter. People in boundary management are most powerful.
- You have to distinguish between short term gains and long term success and sustainability. The path for both may not be aligned, could even be conflicting; one is traded for the other depending on contextual needs.
- Good organizations look for qualities in their employees who work for long term and not those who bargain for stop gap arrangements.
- Honesty and daring to differ if you have a logic based on application of mind, are rewarded. Give unsolicited inputs if you are convinced of its value. Know your industry, organisation, its objectives, priorities, who is what, competitors, happenings in the industry and so on. Develop a wider perspective beyond your immediate call of duty.
- It pays to lose a battle to win a war; aim for long term gains. Detractors and distractions are organisational realities.
- Sense of humour and human relations are important in an organisational context.
- You cannot work in isolation and isolate others from you by your behaviour, that is why there is an organisation.

- Be bold to share your thoughts / knowledge without fear of being usurped by someone. None can take away what is really yours. If you share, others will share too.
- A manager may be designated, but a leader emerges. *Leadership is more than management, leaders stand up to their conviction, beliefs and carry others; managers generally do maintenance. A manager maintains, a leader creates and transforms.*
- Silence is a response as much as a verbal one.
- You don't have to win everywhere; you have to develop your competitors too for the industry to grow!!
- Competitors are not your enemies, they help you to improve by challenging.
- Customer complaints (feedback) is a vital source of information to improve your product / service, never choke this source by discouraging a customer who complains on your service / product.
- Keep your eyes, ears and mind open and be tuned to inputs from the environment. A mind is like a parachute; it works only when it is open.
- Even the junior-most employee has something to contribute, don't create a scary situation around you and drive away people and their valuable contributions.
- You have to respect others as much you want others to respect you and your time.
- Cultural sensitivity is extremely important in *management* as you always deal with people of diversity. What is right and admired in one context may be a *not done*, taboo and even criminal in another; even within the country and outside: ex. dress code, table manners, social etiquette. Be sensitive to manners, greetings, communications, social etiquette of cultures you are exposed to. For instance, consumption of liquor is an offense in some Islamic countries, but an expected social etiquette in the west.
- You have to be sensitive to and comply with organizational policies on smoking, use of organizational resources such as transport, stationery, IT infrastructure, tour expenses, travel guidelines *et al.*

- Qualities desired of you in an organisational context are: reliability, punctuality, honesty, team work, collaboration, flexibility, continuous learning, social skills, acceptable behaviour, handling stress, communication, efficiency, internal and external marketing, accountability and taking on responsibility, enterprising, working towards results, guiding and motivating others, carrying the team, leading from the front, delegation and trusting others but with verification and responsible conduct.

- Emerging traits expectations include business etiquette, negotiating, learning, result orientation, dress sense, telephone and email etiquette, accepting criticism and failures and handling stress.

- Give credit to those to whom it is due. Practise diligent application of mind and not mechanical behaviour, work around obstacles and cultivate a cooperative mentality.

- You have to respect authority, but be alert to limits and trigger points on when to question authority; as you cannot be a blind spectator to undesirable happenings. With a societal responsibility, you may have to question / blow the whistle.

- It is difficult to provide mechanical / logical instructions to handle all possible situations. Individual judgment, thinking on the feet and mustering courage to handle a situation are expected in higher management.

- If you think you can, you will. Cultivate a *can do, will do* and *have done* attitude!

- Cultivate hunger and thirst for success / results, push from within, a mission orientation and a winning streak.

- Personal hygiene helps in feeling good which will feed a positive ambience around, to enjoy your work.

- If you have the courage to explore, you can change the rules of the game.

10

Holistic Value of Cognitive and Affective Traits: Formal Education as a Driver of Success

Stories of self-made icons, rising from nothing, to become the richest in the second most populated democracy and single digit ranking globally, in a span of two generations; Harvard dropouts transforming the globe through innovations in the technology space, interactions with management students, experience of managing fresh recruits (Engineer / MBAs), learnings from the trend of professionals changing track midcareer, MBAs from top institutions shifting to domains unrelated to their education, children of parents in rags topping professional courses - all these lead one to believe mere *good* education, parental affluence and background, access to comforts and convent education do not necessarily shape one's future / guarantee success.

What is extraordinary about these people? Even accomplished academics converge on the divergent definitions of success and low significance of correlation between academic performance and achievements in real life. Does it vindicate those questioning relevance of our education system to meet needs of society? Does it mean education has lost its value as a driver of success?

Recent research explores how the heart and the brain interact in a dynamic relationship, regulating cognitive and emotional experience, neurological signals originating in the heart modulating and influencing brain activities and stress interfering with processes of memory, concentration, judgements, decision-making, creativity and emotions (McCraty). The Heart Rhythm is found to directly influence our physical / mental performance (McCraty 2002). Receiving and having to reconcile mixed signals saps our energy leading to suboptimal performance, indicating the need for *heart* (emotions) and brain (intelligence) working in harmony, for effectiveness in performance. This is evident in the emerging recruitment practices where proven ability to effectively handle dynamic and complex situations is considered the key qualification more than formal education (TheHindu).

Every individual strives for success in whatever goal he is pursuing. Since success is seen to be the synergistic outcome of knowledge base and behavioural elements, attempt is made to expose the *not-so-conspicuous* behavioural elements driving goal achievement. Though it is argued that the individual's personality dispositions to react to situations, determine his destination, it is not clear as to what drives those predispositions. It is likely that life's experience, critical events and a supportive or challenging environment would have catalysed the formation of such personality predispositions. Only potential association is inferred and no causal relationships are concluded from this observation.

11

Gaps in Our Formal Education System

VALUE OF AN MBA

Disappointments confronting MBA graduates when their desire to bag a respectable and lucrative job is not realised, have become the order of the day. It is not unusual to find MBA graduates compelled to accept jobs, considered demeaning when they entered the program. Is there more to an individual's intrinsic qualities to land a lucrative job than an MBA degree? Equally relevant is the growing concern expressed by industry on the low employability of management graduates against expectations. There is conspicuous under-employment among MBAs, high NPAs (Non Performing Assets) from MBAs on educational loans due to poor loan repayment records. Expectation-reality mismatch have led to closure of management schools due to the inability to attract the student community arising from declining value perception. The fact that organisations spend huge resources on training graduates following their recruitment, to scale them up to an acceptable level of employability, tend to make formal education redundant and decline in value perception.

In over-regulated economies, educational institutions lay misplaced emphasis on mechanical compliance with university norms, hardly addressing desired outcomes. To gain market share, enhance foot falls and admissions, educational institutions in private sector adopt strategies to generate hype and visibility among the student community. Focus shifts to showcasing physical infrastructure and the lighter side of campus life to attract student community. Desperate measures to realise short-term business goals in a supply short ecosystem is reinforced by the emergence of a class of institutions that train candidates for employability, offering industry relevant courses. If the parallel institutions are to fill this institution-industry / learning-application gap, how do we justify existence of institutions offering MBA courses under the university system?

The student community realises the true worth of the *degree certificate* when they are about to step out of their *alma mater* in pursuit of a career by when the damage is already done.

EMPLOYABILITY

Employability is the suitability of a potential candidate for employment, on multiple dimensions: technical competency and personal traits. It equally applies to a fresher, a recruit for lateral entry, role change or elevation of an existing employee. The job market is dynamic, reacting to national and global needs.

Few of the requirements for employability pertain to technical skills or competence. Many expectations revolve around affective traits, knowing the candidate as a person, his / her mental make-up. Holistic ability to make things happen along with technical knowledge, attitude, enthusiasm, risk-taking, people skills, maturity, passion and contextual sensitivity mark the employability skills map as shown in the exhibit below.

© Copyright of the University of Kent. Please email Bruce Woodcock, bw@kent.ac.uk if you have suggestions for improvements.
www.kent.ac.uk/careers

WHAT EMPLOYERS LOOK FOR

"A degree can only reflect your mastery of an academic discipline and cannot shed light on your personal skills and qualities. It's the person underneath that counts."

Determination is a key attribute expected of graduates; and for many roles, can be more critical than sheer knowledge. Sometimes referred to as drive: "the determination to get things done, to make things happen and constantly to look for better ways of doing things", ranks sixth in the list of top ten skills that employers want. Determination is measured through surrogates reflecting the individuals' single minded purpose to achieve the goal despite hardships, setbacks, uncertainty, risk …

Determination is closely associated with resilience: the ability to bounce back from setbacks, rather than giving up. When the going gets tough, the tough get going! Perseverance and persistence are related. Determine that the thing can and shall be done, and then we shall find the way. Some of the famous quotes on success / personal traits are presented in the following page.

Famous Quotes on
Success & Personal Traits

Nothing in this world can take the place of persistence. Talent will not; nothing is more common than unsuccessful people with talent. Genius will not; unrewarded genius is almost a proverb. Education will not: the world is full of educated derelicts. Persistence and determination alone are omnipotent - **Calvin Coolidge**

The man who succeeds above his fellows is the one who, early in life, discerns his object and, towards that object, habitually directs his powers. Even genius itself is but fine observation strengthened by fixity of purpose. - **Edward Bulwer-Lytton**

If I find 10,000 ways something won't work, I haven't failed. I am not discouraged, because every wrong attempt discarded is often a step forward - **Thomas Edison**

Commitment is what transforms a promise into reality - **Abraham Lincoln**

Success is not final, failure is not fatal: it is the courage to continue that counts - **Winston Churchill**

I do not think that there is any other quality so essential to success of any kind as the quality of perseverance - **John D. Rockefeller**

Genius is one percent inspiration, and ninety-nine percent perspiration - **Thomas Edison**

Some of the most successful people in the world are the ones who've had the most failures - **Barak Obama**

Develop success from failures. Discouragement and failure are two of the surest stepping stones to success. Most of the important things in the world have been accomplished by people who have kept on trying when there seemed to be no hope at all. The successful man will profit from his mistakes and try again in a different way - **Dale Carnegie**

When fate hands you a lemon, make lemonade - **Dale Carnegie**

Observing the lives of people who have mastered adversity, I have noticed that they have established goals and sought with all their effort to achieve them. From the moment they decided to concentrate all their energies on a specific objective, they began to surmount the most difficult odds - **Dr Ari Kiev**

When the wind of change blows, some build walls, the wise build windmills - **Chinese Proverb**

This Japanese proverb "Nana korobi ya oki" (literally, seven falls, eight getting up) means fall down seven times and get up eight. This speaks of the Japanese concept of resilience. No matter how many times you get knocked down, you get up again - **Daniel Garr (Presentation on Zen)**

The basic difference between an ordinary man and a warrior is that a warrior takes everything as a challenge, while an ordinary man takes everything as a blessing or a curse - **Don Juan (Quoted by Carlos Castaneda)**

Do not fear mistakes. You will know failure. Continue to reach out - **Benjamin Franklin**

The question isn't who is going to let me; it's who is going to stop me - **Ayn Rand**

THE EMPLOYABILITY CONUNDRUM

As per some UN reports, employability of graduates even from elite institutions is becoming a matter of concern world over. Though educational institutions impart functional / technical knowledge, they seem to fail in meeting employer expectations that are beyond knowledge. Knowledge is taken as given for graduates from respected / rated institutions of learning. What employers look for are beyond the obvious *possession of knowledge* by someone holding a certificate (graduation) issued by a credible institution. Employers expect complementary traits in individuals to put their knowledge to work for the benefit of the organisation. These traits are considered to make graduates employable and continue to be employable at higher levels, over time. The visual of an employment advertisement shown below from Airbus says it all.

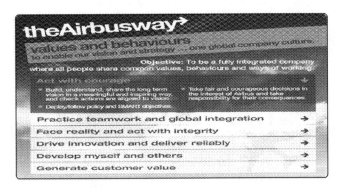

Traits expected from potential employees are values, behaviours, courage to take decisions and act, cultural sensitivity and fitment, alignment to vision, accountability, objective orientation, risk taking, teamwork, innovation, integrity, facing reality and creating customer value. Surprisingly there is no mention of any prescribed technical qualification, years of experience and physical standards. These are taken as given and superfluous to mention.

Mere possession of mandatory technical requirements to qualify for a position doesn't make one employable by Airbus. Mandatory technical requirements are akin to *hygiene* factors; not enough to make one acceptable and succeed. Employability (soft elements of desired behavioural traits) is the motivating factor to make or break the deal. Soft factors are reflections of the underlying potential *enemy within us.* We need to be alert to them and act to ensure that these don't overshadow our positives and become barriers to success.

Test of employability conducted by screening agencies for employment in the technology sector, has four key parameters on which candidates are tested: English Communication, Quantitative, Problem-solving and Computer Science and Programming skills. Of these, communication and problem solving are not technical skills, but are *expected* and carry about 50% of weightage in selection. Overall employability score has been shockingly low for IT product, IT services, BPO and even KPO jobs in India (Employability skills AMCAT 2014). Employability of graduates even shows stark variation across metros from where they come. According to another employability screening organisation, Meritrac, only 21% MBAs were employable as per test conducted in Aug 2012, a fall from 25% in 2007. A study by ASSOCHEM, a national level industry representative body in India, in 2016, has further reduced this figure to a mere 7% (Business Standard).

Stated differently, employability skills and issues are as presented in the charts below.

Employability Skills
1. A set of attributes, skills, knowledge that all labour market participants should possess to ensure they have the capability of being effective in the workplace – to the benefit of themselves, their employer and the wider economy.
2. Non-technical skills which play a significant part in contributing to an individual's effective and successful participation in the work place – referred to as soft skills, generic skills, enabling skills or key competencies
3. Skill sets of a potential candidate perceived by a prospective employer as confirming his overall suitability for employment

Employability Issues
1. According to a World Economic Forum report of March 23, 2010, India to face huge skill gaps due to low employability
2. As per a study by *Purple leap* on employability skill index, only 7% are employable based on a survey of 95 colleges across India, 36% fail on all skills - communication, problem solving, technical skills.
3. Low employability is leading to a cascading effect on colleges whose shakeout is considered overdue and even necessary, if we are to create real value to individuals and the economy from our education system (*Times of India* 2013)
4. Low employability has had a cascading effect on perceived value from education leading to repricing of higher education, demise of capitation fees (a kind of compulsory donation to the institution) and lowered annual fees. The race for quality is evident in faculty salaries and focus on learning outcomes. Campus placement outside the top twenty colleges is a mere 10% (Assocham, an industry representing body at the national level)

5. Of the seven factors listed as wish lists by employers, 78% want employability skills (team working, problem solving, attitudes... all soft elements), the other four elements vary from a low of 2% of respondents to less than 50%

EMPLOYABILITY SKILLS ACROSS COUNTRIES

Relative significance attached to various employability skills across typical countries are listed below. Though there are commonalities and overlaps, *inter se* priorities vary across geographies (cultures).

Australia	United Kingdom
Communication	Honesty and integrity
Teamwork	Basic literacy
Problem-solving	Basic oral communication (e.g. telephone skills)
Initiative and enterprise	Reliability
Planning and organising	Being hardworking and having a good work ethic
Self-management	Numeracy
Learning	A positive, 'can do' attitude
Technology	Punctuality
	Ability to meet deadlines
	Team working and co-operation

The British Council views employment skills somewhat differently, as shown in the chart below.

Employment Skills as per British Council
1. Soft skills are personal attributes that enhance an individual's interactions, job performance and career prospects, unlike hard skills, which are about a person's skills set and ability (technical knowledge and competency)
2. Personality traits, social graces, communication, language, personal habits
3. Graduates, however well qualified, need to be able to demonstrate a set of soft skills.

Hard skills will get you an interview but it is soft skills that get you a job. According to a World Bank funded survey of 200 organisations, the soft skills required are as displayed below.

Core Skills	Communication Skills	Personal Characteristics
Self-confidence	Listening	Business ethics
Critical thinking	Speaking	Professionalism
Creative thinking	Written communication	
Interpersonal skills		
Leadership skills		
Experience with real world problems		

Workplace behavioural expectations are key elements of employability. A variety of aspects of workplace conduct are grouped under four factors as in the charts below

Work Ethics under Four Factors			
Factor 1: *Interpersonal skills, reflected in being*	**Factor 2:** *Initiative, reflected in being*	**Factor 3:** *Dependability, reflected in being*	**Factor 4:** *Reversed attitude/ negative traits, reflected in being*
Courteous	Perceptive	Following directions	Hostile
Friendly	Productive	Following regulations	Rude
Cheerful	Resourceful	Dependable	Selfish
Considerate	Initiating	Reliable	Devious
Pleasant	Ambitious	Careful	Irresponsible
Cooperative	Efficient	Honest	Careless
Helpful	Effective	Punctual	Negligent
Likeable	Enthusiastic		Depressed
Devoted	Dedicated		Tardy
Loyal	Persistent		Apathetic
Well groomed	Accurate		
Patient	Conscientious		
Appreciative	Independent		
Hard working	Adaptable		
Modest	Persevering		
Emotionally stable	Orderly		
Stubborn			

Skills grouped into Three Factors		
Factor 1: Core Employability Skills	**Factor 2: Professional Skills**	**Factor 3: Communication Skills**
Integrity	Identify, formulate, solve technical/ engineering problems	Written communication
Self-discipline	Design system, component, process to meet desired needs	Design & conduct experiments, analyse, interpret data
Reliability	Use appropriate/ modern tools, equipment, technologies	Reading
Self-motivated	Apply knowledge of mathematics, science, engineering	Communication in English
Entrepreneurship Skills	Customer Service Skills	Technical Skills
Teamwork	Knowledge of contemporary issues	Verbal communication
Understands and takes directions for work assignments	Creativity	Basic computer
Willingness to learn		Advanced computer
Flexibility		
Empathy		

12

Life Cycle, Transition, Contrarian Views on Management Concepts and Models

LIFE CYCLE OF BUSINESS OF IDEAS

Management Concepts, Theories and Models go through a life cycle: birth, infancy, growth, maturity, demise or reinventions; similar to tangible products, living organisms and organisations.

Management concepts change their character, gain maturity or are rechristened to be sold as a fresh idea, to gain attention and to serve interests of proponents of these ideas.

On the other hand, some tangible products may get annihilated at the end of their lifecycle, as happened to manual typewriters and Kodak cameras due to emergence of more efficient, low-cost technology driven products, completely eliminating the need for older products.

Obsolescence of management concepts / software products is increasing at a fast pace largely due to the Work in Process (WIP) nature of the ideas / intellectual products masked as final products and sold. This practice is forcing the consumer to pay for and use beta (trial) versions of intellectual products, oblivious of their unfinished nature. The half-life period of new ideas is continuously shrinking, calling for caution in their evaluation and judicious use. One should exercise caution and not be oversold to these ideas.

Beta versions get improvised / bugs get fixed, and are sold as upgrades with or without real additional features or sometimes even rechristened as a completely new product. Examples of such instances of immature products released in the market include several versions of software called MRP and its derivatives (MRP1 – Material Requirement Planning, MRP2 - Manufacturing Resources Planning, CIM – Computer Integrated Manufacturing and graduating to the ERP packages of several versions). Software modules are added on continually and sold as must-have upgradations; ERP packages recast as web-based SAAS products and so on. Such practices of software product developers and vendors call for caution on the part of users while embracing them as innovations.

In effect, the consumer is perennially funding the new development or even the rectification of flaws in products already sold. New versions are gift-wrapped and sold as must have latest tools. Users are also compelled to buy later versions under threat of withdrawal of support to older versions, compulsive licence renewals and so on.

MBA students and management practitioners should recognise that what they are trained to believe as the ultimate, always remain a Work In Process (WIP), and therefore should be sensitive to the true sustainable worth and their remaining useful life of the idea / product transferred.

TRANSITIONS IN MANAGEMENT THEORIES

Management, a subject of social science, evolved in sync with evolution of human society, to meet emerging needs and is an ongoing process. Management theories, models and concepts are distilled narrations of experience of leaders in economic activity, as management primarily concerns with the art / science of managing economic activity. Needs of *Management* are fulfilling needs of economic activity. Many Management concepts and models have their origin in inventing efficient and effective ways of conducting military warfare.

Human society has evolved from a nomadic to agriculture to industry and a service oriented one. Management theories and practices have evolved to meet the needs of these different economic activities evolved over time. In the meantime, many concepts matured from a crude form to high level of sophistication in their application and utilisation, from the industrial to the internet age. Many of these concepts are in the domain of mathematical / scientific models for observation, collection and analysis of data to achieve efficient metric driven scientific solutions. This evolution is a continuous process and ongoing.

Management students and practitioners should be sensitive to this nature of the subject of management and be open to caution, question and examine the scope for improvisation of management practices and concepts. They should exercise their option to challenge and evolve their own methods. It is prudent to resist the temptation to be mechanically guided by top-line headings that may or may not reveal the truth in its entirety, may misrepresent or even present an illusion of a solution masking reality. Prudence should resist the temptation to scout for a drop-down menu box to pick and choose a solution to an ill-conceived problem.

Holistic and incisive approach to problem definition, comprehension, analysis, and solution is the challenge managers face. One should resist tendencies to be guided by halo effect, immediate past experience, proximity bias, preconceived notions, mental blocks and individual limitations.

To illustrate the above, we discuss evolution of management, systems approach, gaps in management education and contrarian views on management concepts, models and practices. These are only to highlight potential damages from applying virgin popular models without critical examination, despite the models appearing to fit the problem.

EVOLUTION OF MANAGEMENT CONCEPTS

Management as a practice and a subject of learning underwent radical changes since the first half of 19th century to the beginning of the 21st century. In essence, Management was seen through two fundamentally different approaches:

- *Mathematical approach*: quantitative, rational analysis
- *Human behaviour approach*: meeting people's emotional and rational needs, recognizing behavioural trends, motivation

A chronological examination of management theories and concepts reveals that they are a distilled and formal narration of practices adopted / attempted, to bring about a scientific (inquiry-based) approach to management of primarily manufacturing enterprises, as illustrated below.

Henri Fayol's Classical Management School

Henri Fayol's (1841-1925) classical management school identifies the principles and skills underlying effective management under "14 principles of Management". Henri Fayol was a French mining engineer, mining executive, author and director of mines who developed a general theory of business administration that is often called Fayolism. He and his colleagues developed this theory independently of scientific management but roughly contemporaneously. Like his contemporary, Frederick Winslow Taylor, he is widely acknowledged as a founder of modern management methods. These encompass the most mundane prerequisites (column 'A') to requirements for orderly organisational functioning (column 'B'), as shown in the chart below.

A	B
Physical: health, vigour	Division of work
Mental: ability to understand, learn, judge	Authority and responsibility
Moral: energy, initiative, loyalty, dignity	Discipline
Educational: knowledge management	Unity of command
Technical: specialist	Unity of direction
Experience	Subordination of individual to general interest

Remuneration of personnel
Centralization
Scalar chain
Order
Equity
Stability of tenure
Initiative and team work

Frederick Taylor's Efficiency Techniques

Efficiency techniques introduced by Frederick Winslow Taylor (1856-1915) comprise measurement of work, worker productivity, and deployment of right kind and right measure of manpower, assessed through granular study of worker's handling tasks (time and motion study), appropriateness of skill and harmonious labour management. Taylor was an American mechanical engineer who sought to improve industrial efficiency. He was one of the first management consultants. Taylor was one of the intellectual leaders of the Efficiency Movement and his ideas, broadly conceived, were highly influential in the Progressive Era. Taylor summed up his efficiency techniques in his 1911 book, *The Principles of Scientific Management.* His pioneering work in applying engineering principles to the work done on the factory floor was instrumental in the creation and development of the branch of engineering that is now known as Industrial Engineering.

Henry Gantt's Charts for Streamlining Complex Tasks

Henry Laurence Gantt's development of 'Gantt Charts' for use in scheduling production and for efficient accomplishment of complex tasks. Gantt was an American mechanical engineer and management consultant who is best known for developing the Gantt chart in the 1910s.

Gilbreths' Fatigue & Motion Studies

Contributions of Frank Gilbreth (1868-1924) and Lillian Gilbreth (1878-1972) that went a long way to recognising need for paying attention to workers' welfare through fatigue & motion studies. Lillian Evelyn Moller Gilbreth was an American psychologist and industrial engineer. One of the first working female engineers holding a Ph.D., she is considered to be the first true industrial/ organizational psychologist. She and her husband Frank Bunker Gilbreth, Sr. were efficiency experts who contributed to the study of industrial engineering in fields such as motion study and human factors. The books, *Cheaper by the Dozen* and *Belles on Their Toes,* tell the story of their family life with their twelve children, and describe how they applied their interest in time and motion study to the organization and daily activities of such a large family.

Charles Babbage's 'Workers' Profit Sharing System'

Charles Babbage's proposal in 1932 that recognized workers as partners in prosperity through a "Profit Sharing System". Charles Babbage was an English polymath. A mathematician, philosopher, inventor and mechanical engineer, Babbage is best remembered for originating the concept of a programmable computer.

Max Weber's Ideas on Corporate Bureaucracy

Max Weber's pioneering ideas on moving towards formalisation of organizational functioning through levels and reporting systems (bureaucracy for large organisations) were adopted by GE and Xerox. Karl Emil Maximilian "Max" Weber was a German sociologist, philosopher, jurist, and political economist whose ideas profoundly influenced social theory and social research. Weber is often cited, with Émile Durkheim and Karl Marx, as among the three founders of sociology.

Mayo Elton's Participatory Management Approach

Recognition of the emotional needs of workers advocated by Mayo Elton in his book, *The Hawthorne Experiment*, led to a shift in approach from mechanistic, to a social worker management, which turned out to be a blow to failure of scientific management. Prof. George Elton Mayo (1880-1949) became famous as the leader in a series of experiments which became one of the great turning-points in management thinking. At the Hawthorne plant of Western Electric, he discovered that job satisfaction increased through employee participation in decisions rather than through short-term incentives. Mayo's importance to management lies in the fact that he established evidence on the value of a management approach and style which, although not necessarily an alternative to FW Taylor's scientific management, presented facts which Taylorites could not ignore.

Peter Drucker Era of Management

The Peter Drucker era of Management focussed on outputs, outcomes and measurement of management functions, accountability of organisations to stakeholders, principles of organizing using activity, decision and relation analysis, federalism, Management by Objectives *et al.* Peter F. Drucker was a writer, professor, management consultant and self-styled "social ecologist," who explored the way human beings organize themselves and interact much the way an ecologist would observe and analyse the biological world. Hailed by *Business Week* as "the man who invented management," Drucker directly influenced a huge number of leaders from a wide range of organizations across all sectors of society. These included GE, IBM, Intel, Procter & Gamble, Girl Scouts of the USA, The Salvation Army, Red Cross, United Farm Workers and several presidential administrations.

SHIFTING PARADIGMS OF ECONOMIC ACTIVITY

During the past two centuries or so, the composition of economic activity has shifted from agriculture to industry and then services. Relative contribution from agriculture, manufacturing and services to GDP underwent major shifts in the last century; conspicuously the swapping of contribution from manufacturing and services; with manufacturing giving way to services. This transition in the nature of predominant economic activities has driven fundamental shifts in management theories and practices.

Agriculture contributing about 48% of GDP in 1840 dropped to about 3% in 2010 and services that contributed to about 32% jumped to 73%. Industry contributed to about 20% with a marginal increase of about 1.5% during the period with a U-shaped behaviour.

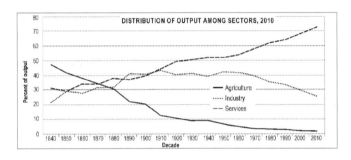

Source: Minnpost, 2012

This led to shifts in internal organisational practices, business practices and also in various functional areas in tune with the evolving composition and character of the economic activities that are managed.

Management was largely seen as a tool to improve efficiency and productivity of tasks undertaken largely with human labour in manufacturing, during the initial phases of the industrial revolution, to generate more and faster out of human resources, to meet demand and withstand competition. The challenge was how to make one's products cheaper and deliver faster for the consumers.

Mass production, mechanisation and automation followed, supported by new possibilities from technological innovations. The profile of human labour shifted from unskilled to semi-skilled and progressively skilled. This led employers to focus on recognising the value of contribution from human knowledge and skill and not limit employee rewards to how agile and hard their muscles were put to use.

Management theories graduated to a means of motivating workers and supervisors to work in teams, bringing their knowledge to the workplace and making them active contributors to achieving business objectives. Theories of organisation structure, autonomy, working in teams, roles and responsibilities, output and productivity measurement, performance incentives recognising contribution from human capital and making employees partners in prosperity, followed.

Internal Practices

- ✓ Management theories evolved from the pre-industrial to the information technology era; matured from an art form based on hunch, to a science, based on data
- ✓ Management as a mult-disciplinary and inter-disciplinary science: recognised the importance of quantitative & qualitative approaches, technology, elements of behavioural science and their interaction, influence and inter-dependency, making it more complex
- ✓ Modern Management is a judicious amalgam of functional and analytical frameworks, productivity / supporting tools and the context of environmental externalities

- ✓ HR practices shifted from protective (benevolence) to competition and productivity paradigms
- ✓ Financial management theory and practices transitioned to innovative business models for financing and benefit-sharing, from the conventional examination of revenues, costs and profits. Private Public Partnership, granular tracking of costs, revenues, budgets, expenses, profitability, monitoring, predictive analysis, forecasting and risk analysis became the norm
- ✓ Accounting (management and statutory) – shifted from *management accounting* to analyse costs, generation of daily balance sheets and P&L statements with compliances as focus. This was driven by stakeholder activism and the need to check potential insider misdemeanours
- ✓ Communication and soft skills – In the internet era, individual employees get exposed to stakeholders from differing cultures and socioeconomic strata. Interactions in a global environment with diverse levels of maturity in the development cycle, nationalities, legal and regulatory jurisdictions, following varying practices and having diverse expectations became essential elements of work place demands. Real time interactions in the virtual world through telephone, email and SMS enhanced the need for sensitivity to business etiquette, competency and risk in a multicultural environment
- ✓ IT driven management, post 1990s, led the shift from managing from single location through face-to-face interaction to virtual offices / virtual organisations,

telecommuting, work from home, just-in-time practices, payment for services at granular levels, tele and video-conferencing as preferred mode of communication and transacting businesses. ERP, CRM, SCM, e-commerce, Business Intelligence, Business analytics, on-demand self-servicing, social networking based marketing, and outsourcing (BPO, KPO, tele-calling, remote services) became the must know elements of the work place lexicon. This transition called for behavioural changes from managers at all levels

Marketing

- ✓ Changing marketing practices based on Point Of Sale (POS) and other forms of advertising to Multi Level Marketing (MLM), Internet / Web marketing, referral mktg. (customer referrals), employee referrals, web links, google adsense and ad-words, online advertisements (to pull customer traffic), online surveys to study consumer behaviour, became the new normal

- ✓ Consumer behaviour tracking and analysis from data in e-commerce sites / social / professional networks, Web 2.0 driven aggregation of individual data from multiple relevant sources ceased to raise eyebrows.

- ✓ Marketing is becoming less and less based on personal contacts and personal influences; calling for a shift in the way we approach it. Marketing should recognise the higher consumer awareness levels, open access to information for consumers, multiple options available for product / service acquisition, competition from unknown quarters including from sources not recognised as competition.

✓ The internet has made the eco-system near-democratic, demolishing monopolies by making access to information and competition ubiquitous, and consumers becoming more demanding

Aspiration Selling

Markets are no longer driven by need to meet basic human needs of food, clothing and shelter. Creation of new business opportunities by pumping up aspirations, and meeting those aspirations are celebrated as innovations. Aspirations are unwanted needs and may not be apparent, but enterprising businesses pump up aspirations that get converted into needs and latent markets. For instance, several personal care products, luxury goods, fashion goods, holiday and leisure travel services, space tourism, grooming and appearance management, entertainment, event management, high-end cars and homes are products of aspiration selling initiatives. These are truly creative, building around a theme, developing products and marketing to those who don't need but aspire for these. Conventional theories on market / demand / competition analysis, demand estimation, etc. don't work here, as there is no base to work from, as these are absolutely non-existent in the present or the past, but are products of imaginative creation.

Management training should emphasise on creative thinking orchestrating multiple elements, in a manner to create competitive barriers, and carve a monopolistic turf for oneself.

Shifting Business Practices

✓ Dis-intermediation enabled largely by technology has blurred organisational boundaries, enabling real time virtual interactions with partners in business; upstream and downstream

✓ Automated loyalty programs, collective purchasing groups, e-commerce, integrated financial services BFSI (Banking Financial Services & Insurance), online trading / banking, learning anytime, anywhere, anything through e-learning are other forms of transition witnessed

✓ Pay-as-you-use through ability to store, retrieve, analyse customer behaviour data at highly granular levels, enable on-the-go packaged offers and dynamic marketing planning covering packaging, pricing, and delivery; upselling and cross selling, deny access to service for non-payment (no bad debts / receivables) and so on

Human Resources: Shifts in HR Management

✓ Labour; one of the three (land, labour and capital) means of production is now recognised as Human Capital. Supervision has given way to empowerment and autonomy. Training cost is now investment in human capital. Penalties and punishments have given way to motivation, total employee care, concepts of employee as shareholder, variable pay and performance incentives, rewards in the form of ownership and employees as autonomous growth partners; policing to trust and independent working, performance measured in the form of efforts (number of hours of work) to performance measured in terms of tangible outputs.

✓ Just-in-time hiring, outsourcing / remote offices / telecommuting, work-from-home, granular performance monitoring and compensation, shift from welfare orientation to opportunities and competition have enhanced exposure and became more demanding

Quality Control

✓ Shifts in nature of businesses and management practices have transformed the way quality is defined and measured. In manufacturing, the product is manufactured, quality is monitored, measured and ensured before delivery to the consumer. In the service industry, production and delivery are co-terminus, by the creator, directly and instantaneously to the customer, without any quality check. Quality check is replaced by quality monitoring through post-delivery feedback from the customer. Customer decides the quality and not the management.

✓ Quality is ensured through systems and processes expected to lead to quality service delivery. High reliance is placed on the service producer for ensuring quality; a shift to trusting the employee for self-certification. The producer is a key element in the chain.

Power-Shift to Producer (Worker)

With the onus of quality on the producer (worker), the producer need to be adequately trained, motivated and compensated and less supervised. The worker knows the end customer more than the management, *de facto* assuming responsibility for delivery. Workers are knowledge workers (several levels above even skilled workers): with differing expectations, at higher levels in Maslow's hierarchy of needs. Worker expects recognition, respect, autonomy, opportunity and competency upgradation, with monetary benefits being only one among the list of expectations, placing complex demands on HR management. Worker being self-managed has led to flat organisational structures and worker participating in decision-making. Even the terminology 'worker (employee)' is rechristened as 'associate' to reflect this changing role, perception and recognition. In this scenario, old tenets of organisational structures, organising and controls will need a metamorphosis.

Disintermediation

✓ Emerging practices enabled by information technology is leading towards a kind of disintermediation, irrelevance of the conventional business organisations, catalysed by crowd sourcing and granular business relationships, direct link between customer and provider of services. Evidences of this trend are several freelancer sites that provide the market place linking producer and consumer / employer and potential employee. Such models demolish the power of large business houses with deep pockets for market reach; the virtual market place platform creating a near equality of all providers bridging the void between a mom-and-pop shop and a global conglomerate providing comparable goods / services. The virtual platforms drive higher levels of democratisation and equal opportunity to all.

✓ The contours of competition space are redrawn, with even large corporates following the mom-and-pop shop trends, to not miss out on the micro and emerging opportunities, even when milking the legacy markets. This trend will catalyse consumerism and entrepreneurship without constraints of legacy, brand visibility, physical barriers, marketing budgets and gestation periods. Corporations have started to read the writing on the wall: recognising power in the hands of entrepreneurs; and even their own competent employees encouraged into entrepreneurship as business partners and not as employees.

Managers should sense these creeping paradigm shifts and their potential impact and the counter measures to guard one's turf or even exploit the new opportunity. The big business now is not making and selling, but are platform providers who never make, stock or even see the goods that traverse their space, but only enable the e-meeting and the transaction. Enablers of business transaction with innovative value additions are evolving as the new power centres; not the ones with deep pockets for capital investment in production, marketing, distribution, inventory, and so on. This power shift brings about new models of management.

Business Valuations

Investment feasibility used to be based on principles of IRR, NPV and Pay-back period. The new trend is betting on the invisible (imaginary) revenue and profit streams expected to be derived from access to (control over) user / customer base. Data on online transaction user base have become the key strength for many businesses with on line presence. Business valuations based on customer data base are betting on the ability to monetise this data base, a second level derivative. Are we moving towards another sub-prime lending bubble?

Are we moving from rational to intuitive decision-making due to poor visibility into the future possibilities except a qualitative expectation? How does one justify such decisions (a kind of gambling) to share-holders without convincing supporting data? How confident and comfortable will the decision-makers be when confronted with such situations? And what would be their accountability?

Business Strategy

Business strategy revolved around identifying opportunities for revenue generation from expansion, diversification, new opportunities and managing competition.

The meaning of strategy has taken a new turn; to mean, actions to identify asset creation for long term monopolistic (developing sticky relationships) revenue opportunities. Asset creation meaning; monopolistic access to markets for inputs and products / services, acquiring businesses for building base for potential sustainable e-commerce revenue, access to natural resources for sustainable long term supply, access to monopolistic technology for conversion into valued goods and services. Businesses look at global sources for strategic control through ownership and rights, even control through open (statements of intent only) collaborations.

What management education should aim at, is developing skills for gaining insights: visibility beyond the obvious, strategically developing competitive positions through innovative means (monopolistic markets for long-term supply to continued use of technical systems, machinery and outsourced services), creating competitive advantage through trade blocks and building dependency through binding contracts, power to withhold knowledge and services. Ability to see / create invisible competitive opportunities will mark the new generation manager.

One of the drivers of identifying market opportunities used to be population growth and GDP growth translated into buying power. This has now translated into gaining granular visibility into shifting composition of demography and markets in each potential market, ratio of productive and dependent population with large proportion of aged / young population offering unique opportunities and constraints.

Global Perspective

Businesses have crossed all national boundaries due to geopolitical changes, shifts in demand scenario, demographic factors, globalisation driven by technology, cross-border competitive advantages, compulsions / opportunities for access to competitive resources, global trade and economic policy agreements, varying regulatory constraints and advantages. A holistic assessment capability is the key vis a vis a single track analytical mind. Synthesis of multiple elements is as important as analytical wizardry. How do we train managers to handle complexity? No one formula will deliver a solution, but an appreciation of the complexity, the dependencies / interconnectedness and judicious orchestration alone will do. The key is integration of multiple elements to make the whole work in a sustainable manner. This needs skills in putting the pieces of the jigsaw together, making meaning out of it, effectively communicating and convincing and delivery skills. The key words are imagination, orchestration, not a mechanical application of prescribed tools.

Political Management

With blurring lines between politics and businesses, managers need to be adept at the art of political selling and diplomacy. There is no one right way that one can learn from a guru, but only sensitivity to the complexity and how one can derive maximum value from it will deliver results.

Many innovations touch multiple sections of society: for instance Internet, Computers and Telecommunications

(ICT). When large and multiple constituencies are involved, it is natural for political attention to gain from the developments. The driving factors are not competition in the market place, but competition for a favourable mind space of the political decision maker. Are MBAs trained on the nuances of political management?

One of the emerging considerations is multi-stakeholder management to gain acceptance. Managers need to be sensitive to what may not appear logical from a businessman's perspective, to get the large constituency buy in; without which initiatives will derail.

Sensitivity to cross-border legalities while operating in multiple geographies. Cross-border operations come with opportunities for gain as well as risks. Managers' ability to sense these will determine outcome of their efforts.

Process Transformation

✓ Functional and organisational structures have given way to process oriented structure, in sync with the logical definition and identification of tasks to be completed, which when integrated, lead to achievement of end-to-end goals. Granular definition and digitising of processes leading to a task completion enable repetitive tasks to be processed using power of Information Technology.

✓ Shift in business environment has resulted in changes in roles and responsibilities, job definition, Key Result Areas (KRAs), performance parameters, performance tracking and appraisals and the entire HR functions. Bill processing and automated payment release for goods and services to suppliers' bank accounts, are linked to organisational budgets. Budget driven financial approvals are automated once the technical approval is in place. This has shifted the auditors' role from auditing transactions to that of auditing the system and focus on process and security.

✓ Customised Performance reports are pulled out from a unique source of transaction data generated at source, any time, not waiting for standard monthly reports and long time lines for generating specific reports. This ensures integrity of data across the organisation, with only a single version of the value for a transaction, event, attribute.

✓ Concept of traditional office timings has become irrelevant as the office is 24 x 365 open, so long as one is connected.

✓ Most transactions including review meetings, presentations, negotiations, inspections are done anytime remotely, with collaboration of persons from multiple locations enhancing ease of team work and pooled form of coordination.

✓ Removal of barriers across organisations that work collaboratively / as partners through data sharing and integrating inputs remotely, through access rights given to individual entities is the norm. Technology has removed barriers of space and time

✓ Above technologically driven changes have led to a new set of issues to be tackled and opened up new opportunities in handling the new set of problems. Emerging regulatory scenario comprises cyber law that makes electronic communications legal and trackable. Data is expected to be retained for defined periods. Data privacy and data protection have become key elements of Cyber laws. Similar business related compliances / legalities include the Sarbanes Oxley Act (SoX) for corporate decision / actions transparency, HIPPA (Health Insurance Privacy and Portability Act), Cross border taxation laws, disclosure requirements, PCI DSS (Payment Card Industry Data Security Standards)

Indian Scenario

Indian scenario is characterised by transition from
- ✓ State-directed > free market economy
- ✓ Welfare-oriented > paying for services
- ✓ Family management (Patriarchal) > professional management
- ✓ Controlled (Restricted) > liberalised
- ✓ Socialistic > calibrated capitalism (free market)
- ✓ Closed economy > open (free market) economy
- ✓ Domestic orientation > globalisation
- ✓ Private sector as a vendor > private sector as partner
- ✓ Low-cost services > value for money (quality services)
- ✓ Low procurement cost > total (life time) cost of operations
- ✓ Focus on rationing > focus on efficiency
- ✓ Supply-driven > demand driven
- ✓ Input monitoring > output measurement, monitoring and acceptance

- ✓ Centralisation > decentralisation (distributed management)
- ✓ Internal focused > entrepreneurial > inclusive
- ✓ Traditional approach (maintenance) > Innovation (development)
- ✓ Customer satisfaction > customer delight (exceeding expectations)
- ✓ Survival > aspirational
- ✓ Follower > emerging leader
- ✓ Isolation > integration with world economy
- ✓ Selling raw material > extracting value from value addition at customer end

MBA students and managers have to recognise these shifts, many of which didn't exist when some of the management books used in MBA programs came into existence. Recognition of these shifts should lead to a practical approach to use of tools learnt in MBA programs.

This gap is also due to the lack of competency of faculty in MBA programs, many of them are from a pre-digital era, and are themselves learning these emerging practices and getting used to the new environment.

Many top MBA programs insist on a minimum of 3-4 years of industry experience as a mandatory pre-qualification for entry into the program. This basic level screening is expected to ensure that candidates carry adequate real-life organisational experience, and thereby competent enough on the fundamental requirements, to most gain from the program.

This many not be true in geographies where candidates enter the MBA program fresh from an undergraduate program and lack the experience to sift, mix and match, tweak the inputs from the MBA program, for its context-specific deployment.

Practice of management calls for continuously reinventing ways to better oneself, and take a call on when to use one's acquired knowledge, how much and in what way and when not to. MBA students should get used to the concept of being on a continuous learning and discovery path.

SYSTEMS APPROACH

A system is a collection of interrelated parts acting together to achieve some goal. It is a set of objects with relationships among the objects and their attributes, related to each other and to the environment and working together. It is a set of independent parts working together in an interrelated manner to accomplish a set of objectives. The key words are *mutual dependency* and *many to many influences*. These influences make the parts elements of a system. The underlying principles of systems approach are described in the following chart.

Underlying Principles of Systems Approach
(a) Holistic view to problem solving
(b) Appropriate problem solving methodology
(c) Multi-dimensional perspective in understanding and analysing problems
(d) Out-scoping the problem definition – stretching beyond the obvious
(e) The belief that there can be multiple Solutions to reach the same objective

(f)	Context-specific appropriateness, while studying relationships
(g)	"Choice" based on available information; we believe that we may have to work with incomplete information
(h)	Recognising fallibility of the decision-maker
(i)	Addresses the problem situation from different angles
(j)	Recognizes interconnectedness of components to arrive at the problem boundary
(k)	Studies dynamic behaviour of the system, not restricted to only one instance
(l)	The approach possesses ability to represent complex system
(m)	Systematic but probabilistic method of analysis and synthesis

Perils of Narrow View

Many management concepts and models adopt a narrow convenient view of the problem and evolve solutions in isolation. However, real-world problems are complex and it is therefore inappropriate to view them in isolation to find practical solutions. This tendency for isolated approach diminishes the value from using these concepts. Isolated approach has led to organisations being structured on functional / divisional basis, with the underlying belief that these functions and divisions had their own independent existence, when in reality they are part of a larger whole and with cross influences.

The emerging *process approach*, to structure work in organisations recognises this interdependency and the friction it can potentially cause, to complete a task end to end, seamlessly. The new approach in structuring work / tasks is to focus on integration, influences, customer orientation and service quality; whereas in the functional / divisional structure, it used to be ease of internal control for management. Focus has shifted from internal control to external (customer) satisfaction and end-to-end efficiency. Technology seems to have enabled and market forces seem to have demanded this shift in approach. Such shifts are pointers to the continuous evolution in management thinking and the need to practise a questioning and open mind to innovate in the practice of management.

Types of Systems

There are two types of systems: Open Systems and Closed Systems. An open system actively interacts with its environment. By interacting with other systems, it establishes exchange relationships. Example: The human mind which influences and gets influenced by happenings in the environment. A closed system is self-contained and isolated from the environment. It is rigid and a non-adaptive system. It does not receive inputs often from other systems and does not trade with the outside world. Example: An automatic wrist watch.

A systems approach completely changes the problem view. How does one see the visual below? One could look at one's role at a very micro level in a narrow sense (as a climber / stone cutter) or one can see the larger space (mountaineer / cathedral builder) within which one's role of climbing or cutting stone is merely an element. The way one sees one's role, shifts the perspective while engaged in a task. A larger perspective helps fulfilment of the larger end objective and motivates teams working in unison to realise desired outcomes. A system also catalyses team work, flexibility, collaboration to tide over surprises and achieve end objective

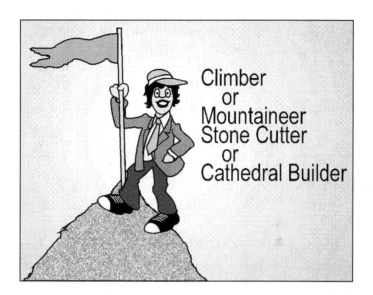

The following exhibit depicts the importance of effective communication and the price to be paid for poor communication. This largely happens when adequate and quality interaction doesn't take place among members involved in a task fulfilment. It reflects one-way dialogue, not a two-way interactive communication. Most failures in projects can be traced to ineffective communication.

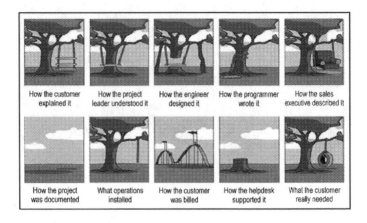

The exhibit below is a representation of how parts when put together constructively (appropriately), result in more than the arithmetic sum of the parts in isolation. In other words, this is demonstration of 'synergy'; where the whole is greater than sum of the parts, depending on how the parts are put together (constructive or destructive). The way subsystems are organised and how they work determine how much value more than sum of their individual parts is created. This additional value is the result of force multiplier. To identify this opportunity for force multiplication, the elements of the system need to be seen through multiple angles and their collective impact evaluated.

Team Work / Force Multiplier

Team work (flying in unison as depicted below or neutralising each-others' energy and efforts) is another classical example of force multiplier depending on how the pieces are put together. This opportunity for value multiplication is not evident when parts are seen in isolation. Force multiplier happens when we work in unison or collaborate to exploit diverse strengths of team members and neutralise individual weaknesses.

Force multiplication (synergy) becomes critical in crisis management and organisational development; pulling all horses together, to gain from collective force of individual horses pulling in sync and in one direction; and not generating a zero sum or even negative sum game by working at cross-purposes. The image below illustrates this.

Systems Approach recognizes the existence of complexity and interconnectedness in management. Holism, multiple external and internal influences on outcomes, *management* as a social system, m*anagement* as open system that is adaptive, dynamic, probabilistic and multi-level and multi-dimensional, are recognised as key elements of effective management in systems approach.

The McKinsey 7 S Model is a formal recognition of this systemic nature of management. The 7s model clearly recognises the importance of the hard and soft elements as in the chart below.

Hard Elements	Soft Elements
Strategy	Shared Values
Structure	Skills
Systems	Style
	Staff

The exhibit below is a depiction of the interdependencies and interconnectedness of these hard and soft elements.

Inter dependencies and interconnectedness are not driven by a pre-coded formula, but are dynamic depending on the context and evolve. This dynamic dependency is due to limitations to our understanding of what drives these dependencies and how as well as the variety of situations that one cannot foresee. This is a recognition of the limitation in our current state of knowledge and need for openness and adopting a systems view.

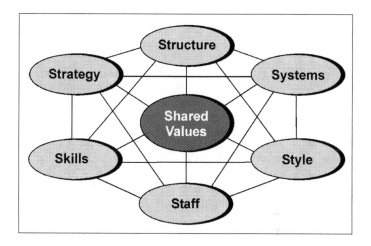

McKinsey 7S Model

The theme of this book addresses the fifth dimension of soft elements: soft elements that are intrinsic to the manager as against the soft elements of the organisation referred to in the 7s model

Contingency or situational approach: holds the belief that actions and outcomes are situation dependent and cannot be predetermined as true for all scenarios. Contingency approach endorses the premises in this book that Management education cannot provide tools and prescriptions for all situations, and the manager has to do the situation driven mix-and-matching job, from among the tools available

GAPS IN MANAGEMENT EDUCATION

Management Course Content, Delivery and Approach

Quality, content and approach of MBA programs to make the MBA graduates relevant to current and emerging needs of business and society is more critical than adding new programs. Business imperatives and market dynamics may drive one to act to appear to be superficially progressive. Grades / marks (internal and external) awarded should be realistic, reflect true competency of the candidate and institutions should refrain from competing among themselves in awarding unrealistic internal grades to enable their candidates to emerge toppers in the university. This would need self-regulation, setting high moral / academic standards and professional integrity among teaching professionals. The day is not far when candidates will be asked who has given the grades and certificates than what grades they have got. Such an unfortunate scenario would reflect falling credibility of the grades as well as the institutions that offer them. This is already visible in candidates from industry acknowledged institutions ranking higher in placement: rewards as well as career growth.

The message is clear as to what employers are interested in: not a rubber stamp and rank award ceremonies but substance. Such a shift towards intrinsic quality will make the candidates better employable; employability being a critical concern.

Doing well what we are doing is more important than doing more. Focus should be on content, relevance, quality, delivery approach and up-gradation than on mere course completion. Competency of teachers should not be judged on their academic qualification obtained in a bygone era from dubious institutions, but their practical experience and currency of knowledge, in order to be able to instil confidence, inspire and generate interest among students and command respect in the classroom. Teachers should have a compulsory period of industry exposure through working in an industry or consulting or other forms of credible involvement, once every five years. Institution-industry collaboration is more important to teachers to make the courses offered and learnings from there brought into the classroom, than for students to manage a job placement upon course completion.

The approach to management education should focus on exposure to real-life aspects of running businesses, understanding of socio-political and economic environment from case studies and debate, understanding, analysis, critique and debate on corporate actions, corporate performance, industry issues, controversies and so on, that are real elements of being in business. Courses should demand demonstrating multidisciplinary approach to understanding, analyzing and finding feasible (not necessarily the one best) solution to business problems. Such solutions should be tested for their outcome and evaluated against the approaches adopted.

Lateral thinking in contrast with incremental approaches is drawing attention due to evolving disruptive concepts and approaches to business, witnessing unbelievable success and paradigm shifts. Conventional definitions of growth are being questioned. Some of the areas needing exposure are: emerging threats and opportunities, latent strengths, business processes, virtual organizations, remote working, outsourcing / in-sourcing / collaboration and e-commerce / ERP / extranet.

Management Education: From Prescription to Discovery

Prescriptive approach to management education leads to diminishing value from education with passage of time. Education should stimulate and catalyse disruptive and exploratory thinking to sync with the dynamic environment. Education should train people to think, analyse, recognise and draw meaning from visible and hidden patterns, innovate and experiment. A prescriptive approach implies that the *past* works for the *present* and will work for the *future.* That may be unrealistic.

CONTRARIAN VIEWS

McDonaldisation: How Far is too Far?

McDonaldisation refers to the practice of over-structuring / standardisation of business practices / processes.

Tracking the evolution of Management theories, it can be seen that, beginning with the classical management school of thought at the turn of the 20th century, *Management* migrated to human-oriented school of thought in the 1920s; decision theory school in the 1950s; innovation-oriented school in the 1970s; Japanese school in the 1980s; eco-management school in the 1990s; and eclectic management school in the 21ˢᵗ century (Holt 1999).

Later developments include technology driven business management practices (not new management theories) post the 1990s, with maturity of information technology, internet, telecommunication and several IT- driven Commercial Off The Shelf (COTS) products.

Postulates of Classical Management

People, Machinery, Raw Materials, Information, Skills, and Financial Capital are considered as organizational assets and Managers are responsible for supervising the use of organizational resources to meet its goals.

Organizational performance defines how efficiently (input to output ratio) and effectively (goal achievement) managers use resources to satisfy customers and achieve business goals. Managerial role essentially comprises four functions: planning, organizing, leading, controlling (Fayol 1984).

Planning is the process used by managers to identify and choose appropriate goals and courses of action for an organization, determining how effective and efficient the organization is and formulating its strategy

Organizing is the process of grouping members, defining working relationships, who does what, accountability, bringing clarity, motivating people and enabling goal achievement.

A leader sets the direction for others to follow for goal attainment, motivates and is accountable to outcome.

Leader need to be enterprising, deterministic, persuasive, goal oriented, fair, dispassionate and knowledgeable to command respect.

Controlling is the process of tracking of activities and progress towards goal achievement and taking corrective steps. This may include performance measurement.

For ease of managing, organizations are divided into levels and divisions or departments, with defined persons assigned at each level and with defined responsibilities and roles (departments): conceptually known as strategic, tactical and operational levels.

Management roles broadly fall into Interpersonal, Informational and Decisional. These three roles are expected to encompass the entire gamut of management, conceptually

McDonaldisation is an outcome of theories of Frederic W Taylor on scientific management, focusing on efficiency, based on close measurement (Harold and Heinz 2012)

Modern management

With the IT revolution post 1970s, *Management* became data driven to meet increasing need for clarity, measurability, predictability, speed and evidence based decisions. Remote operations from centralized control of multi-locational businesses became order of the day.

The next phase of transition was remote monitoring of outputs, hierarchy and structure giving way to cross-border virtual teams and collaboration, flat organizations and technology driven crowd sourcing; role of management shifting to innovation, developing and implementing systems, data analytics, pattern recognition and forecasting.

Day-to-day management support became the task of IT systems, designed around management principles of control, hierarchy, authority, approval, sharing on a need-to-know basis through role based authorisation. Performance data was captured from transaction data, in the background, for monitoring, generating exceptional reporting, alerts and so on. Routine tasks, earlier handled by human intervention are now relegated to technology; human role is to interpret data and its analysis outcome, strategise and decide.

Essentially, management principles and practices still hold, but are obfuscated by the software systems that drive the business operations.

Management practices such as use of technology for Supply Chain Management (SCM), ERP and E-Commerce are built around management principles, but the operations are unobtrusively driven by the software.

Technology-driven business practices such as work-from-home, on-demand service, Just In Time (JIT) procurement, multi-locational collaboration, off-shoring and so on are practices built on core principles.

What have changed are the process of capturing transaction data, its storage, retrieval, analysis, transmission and reuse, at extremely high speeds enabling deeper insights into what the data speaks. Inferences drawn from data analysis enable pattern recognition hitherto impossible. These are used for managerial decisions and crafting radically new possibilities.

McDonaldisation is the unbridled focus on efficiency, metric driven management, predictability and control of outcome. Modern management is driven by the need to be competitive (internally and externally), exercise control over costs, quality, delivery, customer satisfaction and anything, which organisations consider significant for business. With the induction of IT, every activity is defined, tracked and outputs measured. Organisational stakeholders (suppliers, customers, management, employees, shareholders, regulators) expect visibility, traceability, control, defensibility, evidence and predictability in transactions. Emerging business ecosystems expect clarity, definitiveness, adherence to commitments and agreements, visibility; anything that is possible with current technology, to be competitive (Zegre *et al* 2012).

McDonaldisation loses out on effectively handling unique outliers beyond the possible range considered in the design of systems, due to force fitting; an over-simplification for internal compliance. Since such actions take place at the operating levels, lost opportunities may not be visible on the scanner of higher level decision-makers. Incisive competitors may exploit this opportunity through covert use of social media (Denegri and Zwick 2012).

McDonaldisation goes against the grain of adventure (ebayization), variety, experience, uniqueness, personalisation and surprise; expected by certain customer groups, who desire to differentiate and innovate and expect special treatment; when the individual is confronted with a faceless electronic interface. Deliberate creation of non-standardisation is called ebayization (Ahuvia and Izberk 2011)

McDonaldisation leads to loss of qualitative insight, a sub-optimum approach in businesses like consulting and voluntary services, a demotivating factor leading to exits

(Clive *et al* 2005). It is a rationalization process; real humans don't prefer robotic treatment (Ritzer and Stillman 2001).

Acceptance of McDonaldisation approach is culture specific, more accepted in the materialistic west; not in the Confucian east where diffusion (not specificity) is the cultural orientation (Westwood 1997, Ritzer 1996, Babel 2013, Turner 2003).

Preference for made-to-design has been built into the marketing strategy of auto companies to offer customer designed cars (Taylor *et al* 1995), Modernisation deprives the life out of anything lively (Ritzer 2003).

Consumers who are spoilt by personal attention by local businesses resist the impersonal standardisation, characteristic of McDonaldisation. McDonaldisation thus can become a barrier for consumer acceptance, due to the indiscriminate practice of inhuman standardisation (Yamada 2010).

There is an unsubstantiated belief that rationalistic approach in service industry can improve service quality (Levitt 1972), but may not be customer expectations of personalisation and positive surprises

Comments on McDonaldisation

- It is essential to device systems appropriate to different businesses and activities within the businesses, stage of the business and stakeholders, considering possibilities and expectations. Modernisation (indiscriminate adoption of technology driven or technology era practices) based on a mechanistic, one-size-fits-all or many-sizes-fit-many approach of convenience, devoid of sensitivity to holistic needs arrived from granular analysis of trade-offs, could be counterproductive.

- Certain businesses / select activities within them need to do with less of *McDonaldisation*, due to inherent need for openness, flexibility, opportunity for innovation, risk taking, voluntary participation, informality and so on; not to pre-empt access to benefits of non-standardisation (R&D, voluntary services, blue sky innovation, infancy stage of businesses). Great innovations have come from absolutely unstructured work from strange quarters.

- Modernisation deprives one of the comfort of data privacy despite assurances to the contrary. Transparency and traceability are not necessarily desirable in all scenarios; fear of potential exposure can deter participation during exploratory stages of innovations.

- McDonaldisation is good for volume driven matured stage activities: mass production, volume selling and after-sales service for standard products, spread over large geographies, to ensure control, speed, and effectiveness. It is fundamentally suited for mechanistic uniform mass treatment, where personalisation matters less.

- McDonaldisation helps ensure quality, control, feedback, competitiveness, evidence, efficiency, analysis, accountability and predictability, and generates analytics-based policies. However it doesn't provide for being able to see what is not shown.

- McDonaldisation deprives businesses of the opportunity for customization to handle unique situations. This limitation of McDonaldisation need to be recognized in order to not miss opportunities.

- High level of McDonaldisation may tend to drive away customers or lead to forced ill-fitting and dissatisfaction, when exclusivity is expected.

- Indiscriminate McDonaldisation could lead to lost opportunities from perceived inability to be flexible, affecting long-term growth at the cost of short-term internal compliance and convenience. Such an outcome can demotivate super achievers deprived of space for expression and individuality.

- Overuse of McDonaldisation (to handle volume) in Human Resource Management practices, performance appraisal and business development have led to negative consequences from force-fitting and misclassification of performance levels. Undesirable outcomes include exodus of high performers and laggards staying back, lost opportunities due to poor fit of client needs with inflexible offerings. Such negative outcomes could be easily resolved through a discussion and converted into an opportunity, since the losses are due to sheer mechanical mismatch and do not reflect any insurmountable difference. These practice driven limitations and lost opportunities are avoidable with a little imagination. McDonaldisation is liable for misuse by the middle rung staff (those within the two standard deviations band) for personal gain.

- Despite Information Technology being the main driver for McDonaldisation, IT professionals are intolerant to be judged against a standard template. They expect engagement with Management through organic HR practices and are found to promote healthy employee retention.
- Superimposing (topping up) flexibility will not achieve the objective of an intrinsically inflexible system.

Business strategy

Business Strategy defined differently by different proponents, based on what one considers is the key focus of his theory / paradigm / postulate. Examples include

- ✓ Blue ocean strategy that espouses a clean slate approach, out-of-the-box thinking, unbounded by the past, bold, forward- looking and claimed to be superior to other forms of strategy development
- ✓ Porters five forces model of competitiveness, that believes sustainable businesses depend purely on competitiveness driven by the *five forces* of competitiveness
- ✓ SWOT approach where strategy development is driven by an analysis of the past: strengths, weaknesses (constraints) and the future opportunities and threats
- ✓ Systems approach where a holistic integrated approach drives strategy formulation

Contrary to a pigeon-holed approach that individual proponents espouse, strategy is the thinking process in the mind of the strategist (business owner or the CEO). It is not something that is bragged about in public, exhibited on PPTs and broadcast. Such an approach could demolish and neutralize the fundamental premise of a strategy: to take on the competition / adversary by surprise, swiftness and low reaction time for competition, orchestrate unique benefits for the self and entry / operational barriers for others, and continuous evolution to leave the competition / adversary behind (trailing). Strategy keeps evolving all the time in the mind of the driver. Loud statements on strategic expertise brandishing one tool or another are unrealistic, not recognizing the value derived, limitations, need for contextual appropriateness and holism, to deliver practical value.

Real strategy is rarely spoken about loudly other than serving a diluted / text book version, to quench the thirst of analysts. Strategy is more often a game plan residing in the mind of the leader. He may disclose / share elements of it, just as much felt necessary to carry his team along, giving them a sense of belongingness in its conception and implementation, in order to hit the long term agenda. It may also be selectively used for convincing lenders, quenching the thirst of analysts, investors or even regulators.

The question *Can we train one on strategy* is akin to asking can we train someone to be effective? Strategy is individualistic, driven by thinking patterns and thought processes, learnings from experiences, successes, failures and how one has sailed through. Strategy is knowledge interspersed with emotions and the confidence that, one can and the determination to achieve. Strategy is hollow without being different, which is its Unique Selling proposition (USP).

Strategy is impossible without a belief that something that others have not tried or done is possible. Objective of the strategist is to reveal as little of the strategy necessary to give meaning on one's action to those he needs to collaborate with, to achieve his vision.

Stated vision is only a hazy picture of one's mental model of strategy that may never be articulated. Strategy has many elements in the nature of intrigue, bordering on illegality, unethical, surprise and even secretive, which if revealed would derail and endanger goal achievement. It may not even be comprehensible to another. One can comprehend only what is within one's realm of perception. Sometimes there may not even be a strategy, but only a passion that carries one forward. Business school case studies on strategy tend to be more of giving a legitimate meaning to an event from the past, in the language of the strategists, to sync with known theories to gain credibility among social and professional circles. Is it possible to give meaning to all that one does, over another's template?

13

How do We React to Other People's Success?

Our response to situations and the thought process driving our reactions are influenced by our emotional traits and state: beliefs, mind-sets, perceptions, aggressiveness, action orientation; balancing our *need for achievement* and the *fear of failure* (Emotional Competency). Personality traits are intrinsic differences that remain stable throughout most of our life. They are the constant aspects of our individuality (Zimbardo *et al* 2003). These affective elements tend to be more decisive than cognitive knowledge in determining our priorities, response to situations and resoluteness in working towards goal achievement.

Every individual, during his journey, must have been confronted with questions like: Why are some people successful and others not? Why do some fly high, while others apparently similar don't? How much of one's success can be attributed to one's education, pedigree, parental support, family / social background and birth with a silver spoon in the mouth? How do we explain reality defying perceptions on drivers of success? Is there a success formula, or is our understanding skewed or perceptions misplaced?

The American-English form of the trait structure identifies five personality factors as below (Emotional Competency).

Factor	Trait Characteristics	Inverse Trait Characteristics
I Extroversion/ Surgency	Talkative, extrovert	Shy, quiet
	Aggressive, verbal	Introverted, silent
	Sociable, bold	Untalkative, bashful
	Assertive, social	Reserved, withdrawn
	Unrestrained, confident	Timid, unaggressive
II Agreeableness	Sympathetic, kind	Cold, unsympathetic
	Warm, understanding	Unkind, rude
	Soft-hearted, helpful	Harsh, inconsiderate
	Considerate, cooperative	Insensitive, insincere
	Trustful, affectionate	Hard, uncharitable
III Conscientiousness	Organized, neat	Disorganized, disorderly
	Orderly, systematic	Careless, unsystematic
	Efficient, responsible	Inefficient, sloppy
	Precise, thorough	Haphazard, inconsistent
	Practical, dependable	Impractical, negligent
IV Emotional Stability	Unenvious, relaxed	Moody, temperamental
	Unexcitable, patient	Jealous, touchy
	Undemanding, imperturbable	Envious, irritable

		Unselfconscious, uncritical	Fretful, emotional
		Masculine, optimistic	Self-pitying, nervous
V	**Intellect**	Creative, intellectual	Uncreative, unimaginative
		Imaginative, philosophical	Unintellectual, unintelligent
		Artistic, complex	Simple, unreflective
		Inventive, intelligent	Shallow, imperceptive
		Innovative, deep	Unsophisticated, uninquisitive

The chart above on the finer shades of individual personality traits does not lead us to a one-to-one relation between traits and success outcomes. For instance it doesn't answer the question: is cognitive education (subject matter competency) or affective traits (training one's mind to assess and respond to situations) the key success driver?

QUESTIONS WE NEED TO FIND AN ANSWER FOR

Does it need an environment of entrepreneurship one has grown up in, to succeed or is it only a catalyst for success? Is fear, our lack of initiative, low tolerance for ambiguity, risk aversion and low hunger for achievement; the driver for not making an attempt and thereby impeding potential goal attainment? Is it that we don't articulate our goals or lack goal clarity? Cases that defy popular perceptions of why people rise from nowhere, stare us in the face every day. Do these winners have many of the desirable traits for success, even though not conspicuous and not measured?

How often have we felt why we couldn't accomplish what (our close friend, our nemesis, our neighbour, our schoolmate) someone we would have considered very ordinary or even inferior to us in school or college, could accomplish? How often have we felt we could have been better off, but for some missed opportunities? Did we analyse why we missed those opportunities and if we would have handled them differently in a different context? What are the learnings from life's experience - ours and others? Don't we sometimes wonder how, someone who was no one, managed to break the glass ceiling, rise like the Phoenix and get noticed? How do we explain *A* graders in college being surpassed by *C* graders, in real life, college drop-outs becoming industry leaders and global icons making history and even turn into role models in the same institution they dropped out of? Was it the institutions' inability to identify and recognise the valued but latent affective elements, and their over-emphasis on the cognitive traits to rate individual competency, that triggered the dropping-outs?

What is the thought process that crosses our mind when we encounter above scenarios? We tend to justify others' success and our lack of it, by reminding ourselves "if only I were in the same situation or had the same opportunity, I too could have been there and even better". Unfortunately, such thought processes occur after the event and remain as mere possible lessons for the future.

What we fail to recall is that the winner never had the conditions (situation / opportunity) cut out, but he orchestrated the conditions to aid his goal achievement or they fell in place without traceable reasons. Creating *necessary conditions* is part of the process of a winner to goal achievement. This may be called as transformational leadership traits (Hallinger and Heck). Those conditions are not found in text books; neither is there a definitive formula for them. These are contextual, unique to the individual and his / her predispositions to respond to situations and what one considers necessary to achieve one's goal. Responses are driven by contextual factors, *thinking on the feet*, instinct, the uncontrolled urge to get at it, one's own postulates and the determination to do what is needed to make it, unmindful of the consequences and potential conflicts. As a precursor to action, one has already made the choice from among the options and against all odds. One could call it passion.

We cannot recreate a situation that *Bill Gates* had when he set out to create Microsoft, and draw comfort from the argument that I can also do it under those conditions today; since today can never be that day and those conditions can never be replicated in its purity and holism, even to simulate experimental conditions today! Those conditions comprise the tangible and intangible, visible and invisible; and are unique to the individual. May be *Gates* never started with a grand plan that he is going to create a *Microsoft,* that one day will conquer the world. It just evolved after cruising through hills, valleys, headwinds and turbulences during the journey, without notice and oblivious to and uncertain of the outcome. Opportunities surfaced one after the other or were deftly crafted and capitalised on. Passing through turbulence in pursuit of a self-defined goal demands vision, resoluteness and an attitude to overcome the challenges, to reach the destination. This is rarely learnt from text books, but are instilled and internalised through practice, experiential learning, introspection, and self-reinforcement through training one's mind.

14

Can We Be Wiser Before the Event?

Consistently we tend to be wiser after the event. We debate on what stock we should have purchased once we see its price movement! That post-event debate doesn't prepare us for the next similar opportunity, as next opportunity will be argued to be different as we get closer to it and we again retreat from it. This scenario gets re-enacted again and again in a recursive manner, and we refuse to be ejected from this orbit of post-event repentance, due to the strong emotional need to gravitate to our comfort zone.

Windows invaded more than half the planet's homes and offices, *Apple* transformed the personal communication space, *Facebook* redefined the social interaction space and *Twitter* enabled sharing one's thoughts with a community instantaneously. Is it that we have missed the bus for good and cannot create another Microsoft, Apple, Facebook or Twitter? Do we need to follow them or can we not create one for ourselves, may be of a different kind? Did any template exist for the *Gates* of *Windows* or the *Jobs* of *Apple* to follow? Can we not truly *create* (and not look for a formula) what we want to, whose name and character will only evolve as we commence the journey? Many times replicating the past could be counterproductive, we becoming oblivious to the greater latent potential in the present. Copy-cat is never the way to stardom.

Did the icons of today know *a priori* their destination when they started their journey that led to where they are today? Did they know their destination a decade or two in advance? Do they know now where they will be a decade from now? Did they start with a formula or a strategic plan for decades?

Education itself can be a barrier making one to indulge in analysis from past experience leading to paralysis, and forgetting the action essential to achieve results in the present.

15

Action Orientation with Passion

Most achievers possess a child-like optimism, courage (misplaced?) and passion to achieve a secretly nursed goal, a spirit of adventure and hunger for intoxication from the experience. They set off on a journey little knowing the destination, other than the direction, with passion as their only asset. They are willing to experiment, carry optimism, are forward looking, believe in themselves and their goal, are persistent, willing to fail and learn from it. Pursuit of success is a journey; failing (setbacks) being part of that success. They celebrate the learnings from the failures as much as the successes. Nurturing the 'daring to fail' state of mind itself is an achievement, few dare to.

They have to start somewhere, inch through intermediate stopovers to reach a destination they continuously explore: action being more significant than the pursuit of clarity on the path. Analysis should not lead to a state of inaction waiting for the perfect script. Striking judicious balance between pursuit of clarity and action towards the goal determines the outcome.

The tipping point in the balance between *action* and *analysis for clarity* for comfort is driven by individual traits.

This state of the mind will be grey. We can never measure the intensity of clarity and comfort in that greyness in order to compare across individuals. That action orientation approach does not imply lack of direction, planning and a goal. Instead, it highlights the mind of an entrepreneur, a transformational leadership trait, an attitude of risk taking, exploration, spirit of enterprise, treading the unknown path, accepting what unfolds, continuous learning and unlearning, willing to fail and change; a never-say-die attitude, determination with passion, enjoying the process and steering the way. It simply means unbridled internal clarity, focus and determination on goal achievement as the superordinate goal; *means or the path* being subordinate to the *end*.

These traits are never visible or measured across individuals. These achievers will never have all the resources, name and fame at their command nor know all pieces of the puzzle and how they would fit in, when they set out on their journey. This state of dilemma need not signify end of the road for those who could not be one of these icons?

16

Mind of the Entrepreneur

An entrepreneur is one with a never-say-die attitude, daring to pursue a goal, owning no resources except the passion and determination to achieve, getting up and start walking every time he falls. He is not the one to give up. He realises that the future always evolves despite the strategic planning tools and techniques, mastered in business schools. Real world is a test of our ability to comprehend complexity, confront uncertainty, risk, fail and learn from it and never give up. It is driven by a deep-rooted belief that one can achieve what one set out to, despite successive setbacks, reaching a point of refusal to learn (change one's belief).

Negative experiences are only viewed as lessons to be learnt and never allowed to distract one from the set goal. Is this the optimism of a punter? Should we choose to refuse to learn from failures? May be! The adage *If you think you can, you will. If you think you may; you will never,* may be a reminder for fence sitters. Did anyone imagine America will ever be led by a black of African Muslim origin, post the 26/11 bombing attributed to the Islamic world?

The world is available for anyone who wants to make what he wants out of it? Achievers design and create their own destiny, not mimic a winner they look up to, as a role model, but learn from them to pursue own path, choosing what they want to be and make icons of themselves. They consciously allow others to mimic them in order to capitalise on their own mistakes from mimicking.

The intent of this discussion is to reinforce the belief that beyond intelligence, birth, inheritance, luck and opportune time, there is something very unique to one's mind that drives one's destiny. Success and achievement are more to do with one's *heart* and less to do with the *brain*. Those with the right heart will relentlessly pursue, gain access to the brains needed to give shape to their dreams.

Failures help in seasoning and hardening. Those who have failed are more likely to pursue a path to success; never giving up until reaching the destination; continuously shifting the goal post, raising own standards and achieving them. Distant observers may not even comprehend where they are going, till they reach their undisclosed destination. They are seen only when they have arrived, they do not announce their ETA (Expected Time of Arrival). They are the silent achievers, valuing only the outcome. Pursuit of their goal makes them oblivious, immune and insensitive to the pains. They promise less and perform more. On-lookers find them deviants and mavericks, poorly aligning with social norms; may even be ostracised from their groups, as they make a poor fit!

Some of the top management programs consciously look for participants who have failed and risen from the grave, as there is no other proven way to assess the *true* qualities of an individual to be eligible to participate. Such participants invigorate the group from sharing their own experience and having lived through failures. Living with those who have lived through turbulence is the greatest convincing experience and motivation for others to learn from. Candidate assessment for some MBA programs expect successful candidates to have demonstrated entrepreneurship and experienced failures.

17

Mavericks as Change Agents

Entrepreneurs are different! To be different is no crime. To be different is to dare and be creative. We wouldn't have had the gadgets we enjoy today, if there weren't mavericks (crazy minds) before us to create these. How crazy would it have been to imagine half a century ago that the world will communicate over space, instantaneously at no cost as we enjoy today. Don't we need crazy minds over conformists, to imagine the near impossible, to take us to new experiences?

It is easy to agree but difficult to disagree and stay there. One should choose the difficult path, to get intoxicated from the experience of challenging, failing, achieving; qualities that set apart creators from the also-rans. How many of us are ready to take the risk of failure, rejection, potential of being charged for sedition, leaking state secrets, challenging norms / accepted practices when we don't have to? Can we progress if we continue to be just compliant? How many of us dare to stray away from our comfort zone of social acceptance and occasional eulogy? Change can only be brought about by revolutionary thinkers branded as *mavericks*.

One need not emulate others' path, but may learn from them to chart one's own path. One needs imagination, dare to think crazy, be different, be branded a maverick, walk solo and be humble every time they reach their next goalpost, only to shift it further. An outsider may believe they are punishing themselves; but they are enjoying the process of failure, discovery and success; only to replay again. They are the serial entrepreneurs!

Do we encourage and create mavericks? Do we need to train people to think unconventional and design the unthinkable? Is thinking an art unique to an individual or can people be trained to think? Is there a method in the madness? 'Design Thinking' is already an academic discipline being pursued by product designers in the technology space.

Is there a lesson for students of management from these recent events from history? Can we try to understand the mind of these *special characters*? Can we motivate the student community to introspect and ask the questions: Do I aspire to be one? Can I be that one? Do I have to? What if I don't?

18

Thoughts on Success

1. If one has never failed, one hasn't done anything worthy of celebrating the success. Only one who dares to walk can slip and not a sleeping one. Those who haven't made mistakes have rarely attempted anything; it means one hasn't pushed oneself to the edge. There is nothing as exciting as being-on-the-edge. Success / achievement that come without pain / risk / fear is not success. Fear is a good experience, so is bad experience. Nothing can substitute the experience of near drowning in a pool. There is opportunity in every crisis. Success can take many forms and shapes. Forms and shapes are immaterial, achieving them is. To succeed, one needs *achievement orientation*.

2. If we want to see something we will see. If not, we will be blind to what is in front of us even with a healthy vision. We see and hear only when our mind is open, not because one has good eyes or functioning ears. Mind is like a parachute, it works only when it is open. Keep your mind open. You will be able to see opportunities invisible to others

3. If someone is criticising you, it means he finds you worthy of competing with. The worst punishment is being ignored. Respect your rival as you consider him worthy of being taken note of (worried about?). Encourage and learn from competitors, competition is the essential driver to excellence.

4. When you start getting too comfortable with something (career, earnings, social status and circles) it is time to remind yourself to look elsewhere or change; a prolonged state of comfort is the beginning of the end. Too much comfort implies you are not challenged; not being challenged reflects a state of complacency and others considering you not worthy of challenging; the beginning of degradation and the end. Push yourself to the edge and experience the adrenaline rush.

5. To be matured, one should experience the *highs* and *lows*. *Lows* are the catalysts for seasoning and ruggedizing, leading to maturity. The *highs* help relax and ponder, not to get excited. Humility is strength and not a weakness, a manifestation of confidence, not inferiority.

6. Do not judge a person by his/ her looks (or a book by its wrapper); like the depth of a river to assess its safety to cross, by its average depth!

7. Challenge yourself to surpass your own standards. Be your own competitor and set standards for others. That gives you a front runner advantage without being charged for *insider trading*.

8. What happens when you differ? You break out of the mould to exercise your independent thinking and expressing yourself; get ridiculed and criticised; you may not find acceptance in your immediate circles, who are used to seeing you in a mould of their making. When you pursue your new path, you initially get ridiculed, then observed and finally followed. Every invention or change is the work of someone who dared to break out of the mould; who chose to walk the path solo and enjoyed being followed when others found value from you being *different and your way*. All great men were once considered mavericks, punished for being different; some became heroes while some perished. You don't gain anything by being a blind follower, out of fear or for the comfort of being in agreement and eulogised in close circles. Do what you enjoy doing, to excel.

9. Some basic principles to follow, when in doubt, may be in order. These are like superordinate goals, suggesting the line of action / considerations guiding your decision, when confronted with situations pulling you in conflicting directions or when you are in a dilemma. Superordinate goals are deep rooted and superseding everything else. We have had situations when we had to choose one over another, though both may be seen as equally important / right in isolation; or in a different situation where a choice either way would be subject of criticism. Ability to effectively handle conflicting situations under scrutiny and criticism is the mark of maturity and self-confidence. Coming out unscathed boosts confidence and hunger for more. Recall the

celebration of war heroes when they are welcomed back from the theatre of action.

10. Know yourself and your value. Never sell yourself cheap. If you don't quote your price no one will. You are what you think you are, not what others speak about you in your presence or behind you.

11. To be rejected is no shame, may be you didn't lose. It was a blessing in disguise and those who couldn't find value in you lost. May be they were less than comfortable to have someone more qualified and of higher competence like you, amongst them. They would have seen you as a threat!

12. No man has ever died of hard work. For many great men, work is the intoxicant that keeps them mentally and physically active and healthy; and helps maintain their social status, economic freedom and self-esteem.

13. Never trust someone showering praise on you; beware of hidden agenda. The most potent weapon to destroy someone is to shower praise, so that he drowns himself in a state of blindness, complacency and misplaced euphoria. So also are attempts made to intimidate you or shake your belief in the self, your self-esteem and self-confidence. Be first yourself and for you.

14. Successes from short-cuts have short life, like being a king in a village. When you get exposed to a larger space and competition, your real worth gets exposed. Expose yourself to competition. Competition alone drives you

to excel. All innovations have their roots in competition and hunger for growth and survival

15. Our biggest enemy is our diffidence, losing focus and dissipating our energy in unproductive directions, over-dependence on soothsayers, belief that some divine miracle will solve our problems. Cultivate the ability to see the method in the madness and practice order-in-disorder. These enhance one's understanding and confidence level.

16. To be selfish is no crime; it is criminal to pretend to be philanthropic, and self-destruction to take beatings for another. Some get fooled by another's magnanimity to come to their rescue. Remember your distress can be someone's opportunity. Accepting unexplained magnanimity creates obligations, emotional bonding (dependency / slavery) and loss of freedom to pursue larger objectives. Your low could be just a blip, but the temporal unhealthy bonding with your saviour could be disastrous for long. There are no failures in life, only setbacks. While failures are irreversible, setbacks are transient. Let not the setbacks snowball into a failure

17. Everyone wants to be safe, secure and avoid risk. The biggest market is for safety and security; that is why insurance firms thrive on people's scramble for safety. Risk and returns are positively correlated. You can expect returns only if you venture into the unknown space (risk). That is why there are few leaders (who venture) and large followers (preferring safer zones). If

you have to be above the crowd, risk venturing into the unknown space. It pays.

18. One man's food is another's poison. Do not believe that someone's path to success is the right one for you. May be you have a better one in store; look for it. We are more comfortable to follow someone; few dare to lead change as change causes discomfort of various kinds, puts you on the defence, having to explain your position to even the insignificant others. Many tend to avoid it. Remember, satisfying someone else is not your goal in life. First satisfy yourself. Playing second fiddle is different from leading from the front.

19. One learns from failures, success only blinds. Every failure leads to introspection and reflection; the most effective form of learning and internalisation.

20. There is no substitute to the joy of success after a failure! The more you fail before you succeed, higher is the value and joy of success. Learning from failure can never be taught in a classroom. It is highly personal and emotional and has to be self-learnt by going through the process. It cannot be transferred to another in its entirety and purity. Many corporations scramble to recruit failed entrepreneurs, as entrepreneurship is deep-rooted in the individual and cannot be transplanted. As an entrepreneur never gives up, shrewd employers take him for his persistence and entrepreneurial attitude in difficult situations.

21. Thin line divides confidence and arrogance. So are innovation/enterprise/initiative and illegality; the hero

and criminal. Your confidence could be arrogance for those who are used to sycophancy and sooth saying. Do not buckle under pressure to buy peace or draw comfort from acceptance or even eulogy. It is not worth the price you pay by selling your future and your freedom; striving for acceptance. Potential leaders are generally not accepted as good followers, as expectations are different for the two roles

22. Creating favourable public opinion (PR, advocacy, lobbying, marketing, intrigue) is part of every successful entrepreneur's job. Creating conditions for success for followers is the most critical task of a leader. These are orchestrated through lobbying, opinion leadership and policy advocacy using methods fair and foul, intrigue not being a taboo. Most CEOs in large corporations spend significant resources on boundary management, political management and environmental management. Dividing line between the *right* and *wrong* gets thinner and even overlap bordering on conflict of interest / illegality.

23. Dare to question even the authority, as claimed authority could be usurped or transgressed authority used for gain. Right and wrong are relative. Successful one is the one who can make the *wrong* look *right*. Communication, persuasion, orchestration, force or even intrigue are strategies adopted to right the wrong

24. Not taking risk is the biggest risk, though the nature, severity and consequences may vary. By not taking risk, you may be paying someone a premium for shielding you

from the risk, from which you are not fully insulated, though you may be led into an illusion of safety. You only trade risk for the returns of an apparent emotional temporal comfort, for which you pay a disproportionate price.

25. Take the bull by the horns, few have the guts to do so, but returns are highest in doing so. Side-tracking an issue will not eliminate it. You save a lot by directly dealing with it than attempting evasive tactics or soft pedalling. Leadership is also the courage to expose oneself. Demonstrate your leadership when an opportunity arises.

26. Every idea has a right time; many great minds were crucified because they were before time. Be alert and sensitive to writings on the wall.

27. If you do 99% and drop off (abandon your project / pursuit), someone else will do the last (1%) mile and take credit for the 100%. Never leave something without seeing its logical end, else you will become someone else's unpaid worker, as that someone will find value in the scrap you have left, and extract gold from it, as you didn't have the perseverance. Conviction, persistence and perseverance are critical emotional traits of winners

28. Practice continuous learning, unlearn and relearn. Knowledge has evolved over time, concepts and principles (of management) have undergone paradigm shifts. One needs to be open to recast one's knowledge base with changing times.

19

Helpful Practices for Effectiveness

1. Have an open mind and enjoy your work and life. Openness is a positive state of mind to receive another's ideas/views. People like to be heard!

2. Keep physically and emotionally fit, be sensitive to personal hygiene. It helps to exude confidence, positive energy, acceptability, participation and getting people to action

3. Build and maintain professional and social network. Don't burn your bridges behind you. You may need to retrace the path to pursue relationships under a different paradigm, after decades of separation and silence. Recall how school and college alumni re-establish old contacts as if they were together the previous evening. Alumni networks break all barriers.

4. Life comes as a package. Do not try to pick and choose within the package. There are no garbage collectors to pick what you choose to discard

5. Believe in yourself, have a can do and will do attitude. This helps in mobilising participation

6. Dare to fail, enjoy challenges and learn from failures. It gives you the adrenaline rush to face challenges

7. Be simple, humble, young in mind, open to learning from generations Y / X. By practising this you never go outdated, but gain confidence and will be better accepted

8. Look forward to the best and be prepared for the worst. It reflects neither gullibility nor pessimism, but reality

9. Believe that there is no one right way, there can be many. It helps generate diverse ideas for efficient problem solving

10. Opportunities exist at all times for everyone. Have an open eye, ear and mind to grab it. You see only when your mind is open.

11. Adaptability is not lack of direction. Understand the fine distinction between focus and flexibility, they are not antonyms

12. Believe you have lot to give and take from others; share, as none can steal what is yours. If you share, others will reciprocate

13. Human beings are basically good; circumstances make them what they are. Understanding what made them

who they are, makes you more humane and help you to get the best out of others

14. If you challenge someone, be prepared to get injured. There is no one-way traffic

15. Life can begin at any time if you want it that way; it is never too late. Do not blame age or others for your lack of initiative

20

Essential Qualities for a Successful Leader

1. Self confidence

2. Honesty, not hypocrisy and integrity ultimately pay

3. Take failures (setbacks) as fact of life and don't accept them lying down

4. When someone laughs at you, laugh with them. You will completely redraw the contextual map and be in control of the situation

5. Have the competitive spirit of a sportsman and resoluteness of a general

6. Be able to see (vision) what is not visible. Not many can. Those who can, are a class apart

7. You can't and don't have to correct everyone, correct yourself

8. See the world in all its manifestations, gain confidence and courage to face it. Variety is not only fact of life but equally essential. The rich cannot have their good life, without the poor to provide them services essential to enjoy their good life

9. Believe you are no less than anyone else and you need to excel in what you take up. Do not be content with sloganeering and hollow displays. Truth and competence will ultimately prevail

10. If you have to challenge *status quo*, do it here and now, as there is no tomorrow. Challenge is the driver of change. Majority need not be right always.

11. No one needs sympathy, people need empathy and someone to share their mind with

12. There is no level playing field in real world, if it was so, you would have to rewrite books on core competency, SWOT, competitive advantages of nations and so on. Clamour for level playing field is, in fact, seeking that differentiator surreptitiously, by those who lobby for it under the banner of level playing.

13. Enjoying good life that you have earned is no crime. One can enjoy in different ways, not necessarily through displayed consumerism

14. Happiness is an inner state of the mind; not a display of grand life

15. There is no real charity; even charity comes with a hidden price or a deferred return. Hidden agenda is part of life

16. Develop right attitudes, values and practices, nurture a quality culture

17. Be bold to state facts, hold your ground even at a price

18. Don't look for short-term gains, they don't stay. Satisfy yourself before you try to satisfy others. Don't wait for an inspector to right the wrong. The earlier you correct, the less expensive it will be

19. Set high standards in all that you are involved

20. Believe *you can* and *you will*, you will

21. There are no failures in life only transient setbacks, so never lose your composure when you don't get what you are after

22. The day you find yourself comfortable on a job, it is time you start introspecting if something is wrong and you need to move on. The feeling of comfort is a slow poison, it is a stumbling block to progress, as there is nothing you see challenging. You are underutilized and need to find a new space where you can exploit your potential

21

Reality Check for MBA Freshers

1. There is no real level playing field (as clamored for by industry associations). Every field is uneven, you need to take advantage of the uneven terrain and compete. Create your own USP (Porter 1990, Golf). Competitive advantages are many times contextual and unique to individuals and organizations.

2. Managers are designated, but leaders emerge. Leadership is beyond management; leaders stand up to their conviction, beliefs and carry others; managers manage others. A manager maintains while a leader creates. Organisations look for leaders (Murphy 2006, Peters 1985, Reeves 1998, Prahlad 2006).

3. Wisdom is good learning from bad experience; inexplicable; may appear illogical, defensive, and not youthful; but are time-tested, and yield long term value. Intuition and instinct are wisdom in action

4. Children are most innovative, since they are not conditioned by the past experience. Experience can be

a barrier for innovation and discovery. Innocent greenfield approach may yield great rewards, as evidenced in recent times in the technology space. One has to continuously question *status quo*, to progress over a different paradigm.

5. There is light in every dark room. It is our inability to see it that makes one give up.

6. Fear of the unknown is less for the ignorant. Information overload can be a barrier; we tend to imagine non-existent problems / risks.

7. Even the junior most employee has something to contribute; don't create a scary situation around you, drive away people and silence them. They will speak to your competitor

8. Be sensitive to and comply with organizational policies on smoking, use of resources such as transport, stationery, IT infrastructure, tour expenses, travel guidelines. It enhances others' perception of you as responsible. Small misadventures may come with a heavy price.

9. Qualities desired: Reliability, punctuality, honesty, team work, collaboration, flexibility, learning, social skills, acceptable behavior, stress management, communication, efficiency, internal and external marketing, accountability, enterprising, working towards results, guiding and motivating others, carrying the team, lead from the front, delegating, trusting others but with verification and responsible conduct

10. Give credit to those to whom it is due, practice diligent application of mind and not a mechanical behavior, working around obstacles and a co-operative mentality

11. Bottom line is, you will be rewarded for what you deliver; all your other shortcomings will be condoned. Focus on creating value and deliver. Any organisation needs lateral (mavericks) thinkers, not just those who follow the crowd. If you have to create an Unique Selling Proposition (USP), you have to be different!

12. All happenings in life cannot be logically explained! You will find instances where outcomes defy logic. Have an element of instinct and intuition. Life is not mathematical, as the logic of the logic is undefined and differs across individuals.

13. Success is not defined on one yardstick, there are many and there can be many measures of success and achievement. It depends on the individual seeking the goal.

14. Organisations and leaders have committed blunders. Most failures / blunders do not surface or draw adverse attention; only because successes have, over a period of time, overshadowed failures or failures have been effectively managed from surfacing and exposure (obfuscated). You will also reach a stage when your pluses will be more than minuses. Ultimately it is a balance sheet. Sometimes successes are managed by masking failures!

15. Happiness is a state of the mind and cannot be measured on a scale. In retrospect, you may ridicule your own celebrated wins! That is maturity

16. Silence is a great message. Silence is not *no response.* Many times *no message* is the right message. To be a good speaker / effective you don't have to speak more; it is like Golf - a thinking man's game. You can have all the shots in the bag, but if you don't know what to do with them, you've got troubles. It is like mental golf; you need more thinking before action, you need to know your end objective and plan to reach that, ignoring the intermediate setbacks.

17. Collectivism and individualism: While western societies are generally individualistic, eastern societies are collectivist in their orientation, mores and social norms. Collectivist societies tend to force individuals to fall in line with the *supposed collective decisions.* Individual opinions and views, being different, thinking out-of-the-box or obtrusive expressions are not appreciated; and may result in admonishment or rejection by the group. In such societies, individuals may have to adopt strategies that are tantamount to hypocrisy. For instance, it may be (politically) wise to appear to be dumber than what you really are. In a collectivist society, one therefore need to be socially intelligent to pursue one's goals through unobtrusive means, in contrast with the western world; where loud expression is appreciated, expected and considered as reflecting a person's capability and confidence. Such behaviour

though illogical, is the norm in these societies. One needs to manoeuvre one's trajectory through means that may amount to obfuscation, portrayals, deceit, masking and so on. One should be able to withstand social pressures in pursuit of achieving long term goal.

One has to strike a fine dynamic balance between being inside the *collective group* and secretly preserving one's individualism, in pursuit of long term goals. Even in collectivist societies, a minority deftly take leadership positions and are highly individualistic, portraying an image of brotherhood in the collective society. Maintaining such split personality is an art. Leadership demands goal orientation and someone piloting it.

In such societies one cannot afford to be obtrusively individualistic, as such a conduct may invite hostility and impediments to one's progress. One has to play a double game and following own path deftly.

22

References

1. Ahuvia, Aaron; Izberk-Bilgin, Elif; Dec 2011; Limits of the McDonaldization thesis: eBayization and ascendant trends in post-industrial consumer culture; Consumption, Markets & Culture; Vol. 14 Issue 4, p361-384. 24p

2. Babel, 'Seven Dimensions of Culture' available from www.babelgroup.co.uk, [Dec 29th 2013]

3. Brainpages available at http://brainpages.org/whats-the-difference-between-the-mind-and-the-brain/

4. Business Standard available at http://www. business-standard.com/article/pti-stories/only-7-of-indias-b-school-graduates-employable-study-116042700584 1.html

5. Clive Nancarrow; Jason Vir; Andy Barker; Ritzer's; 2005; McDonaldization and applied qualitative marketing research; Qualitative Market Research: An International Journal; Vol. 8 Issue 3, p296-311. 16p

6. Controlmind available at http://controlmind.info/human-brain/the-difference-between-brain-and-mind

7. Cultural dimensions of management available at https://www.primeconsultinggroup.in/wp-content/uploads/2015/07/cultural dimensions_of_management_-_china_vs_France-2.doc

8. Denegri-Knott, Janice; Zwick, Detlev; Apr 2012; Tracking Prosumption Work on eBay: Reproduction of Desire and the Challenge of Slow Re-McDonaldization; American Behavioral Scientist; Vol. 56 Issue 4, p439-458. 20p

9. Emotional Competency available at http://www.emotionalcompetency.com/personality%20traits.htm

10. Employability skills AMCAT; National Employability Study by Aspiring Minds: AMCAT scores of more than 120,000 technical graduates engineering and MCA students (in final year) across the country, in more than 20 states for year 2014

11. Fayol Henri; 1984; General and Industrial Management, revised by Irwin Gray, London: Pitman

12. Gantt, L.Henry (1861-1919)

13. Golf, available at http://www.gorillagolfblog.com/opinion/why-golf-is-the-thinking-person%E2%80%99s-game/

14. Hallinger, P. And Heck, R.H. (1998), "Exploring The Principal's Contribution To School Effectiveness: 1980-1995", School Effectiveness And School Improvement, Vol. 9 No. 2, Pp. 157-91

15. Hamel, Gary, and Prahalad C.K Competing for the Future. Harvard Business School Press, 1994

16. Harold Koontz and Heinz Weihrich; 2012; Essentials of management, An International and leadership perspective, 9th Edition, Tata Mc Graw Hill

17. Holt, Knut; Mar 99; Management and organization through 100 years; Technovation; Vol. 19 Issue 3, p135. 6p. 1 Black and White Photograph

18. Indian college dropouts available at http://www.siliconindia.com/news/business/6-Indian-College-Dropouts-Who-Are-Now-Billionaires-nid-153350-cid-3.html

19. Leithwood, K. And Jantzi, D. (1999), "Transformational Leadership Effects: A Replication", School Effectiveness And School Improvement, Vol. 4 No. 10, Pp. 451-79

20. Levitt, Theodore; Sep/Oct 72; Production-line approach to service; Harvard Business Review., Vol. 50 Issue 5, p41-52. 12p

21. McCraty R (2002), Influence of Cardiac Afferent Input on Heart-Brain Synchronization and Cognitive

Performance. International Journal of Psychophysiology; 45(1-2):72-73

22. McCraty Rollin - The relationship between heart-brain dynamics, positive emotions, coherence, optimal health and cognitive function in http://www. coherenceinhealth.nl/usr-data/general/verslagen/ Verlsag_Rollin_McCraty.pdf

23. McKinsey 7S Model available at https://www.mindtools. com/pages/article/newSTR 91.htm

24. Mindbrain available at http://www.differencebetween. net/science/health/difference-between-mind-and-brain/

25. Minnpost available at http://www.minnpost. com/macromicro-minnesota/2012/02/ history-lessonsunderstanding-decline-manufacturing

26. Murphy, J., Elliott, S., Goldring, E. And Porter, A. (2006), Learning-Centered Leadership: A Conceptual Foundation, Learning Sciences Institute, Vanderbilt University, Nashville, Tn

27. Peters, T. And Austin, N. (1985), A Passion For Excellence: The Leadership Difference, Collins, London

28. Porter E Michael., 1990, Competitive Advantage of Nations, Free Press - Business & Economics

29. Prahalad, C. K. 2006, The Fortune at the Bottom of the Pyramid, Pearson Prentice Hall - Business & Economics

30. Reeves, 1998, Leadership & Organization Development Journal 19/2 [1998] 97–105 © Mcb University Press [Issn 0143-7739], Leadership For Socially Responsible Organizations, Richard H. Reeves-Ellington School Of Management, Binghamton University, Binghamton, Ny, Usa

31. Ritzer, George; Oct 2003; Islands of the Living Dead: The Social Geography of McDonaldization; American Behavioral Scientist; Vol. 47 Issue 2, p119-136. 17p

32. Ritzer, George; Sep 96; The McDonaldization Thesis: Is expansion inveitable?; International Sociology; Vol. 11 Issue 3, p291-308. 18p

33. Ritzer, George; Stillman, Todd; Apr-Jun 2001; The Postmodern Ballpark as a Leisure Setting: Enchantment and Simulated De-McDonaldization; Leisure Sciences; Vol. 23 Issue 2, p99-113. 15p

34. Taylor, Stephen; Phil Lyon; Lyon, Phil; 1995; Paradigm lost: the rise and fall of McDonaldization; International Journal of Contemporary Hospitality Management; Vol. 7 Issue 2/3, p64. 5p. 4 Diagrams

35. The Hindu available at http://www.thehindubusinessline. com/industry-and-economy/logistics/want-people-whove-learnt-from-life-says-airasia-india-chief-mittu-chandilya/article6701664.ece

36. Turner, Bryan S; Oct 2003; McDonaldization: Linearity and Liquidity in Consumer Cultures; American Behavioral Scientist; Vol. 47 Issue 2, p137-153. 17p

37. Westwood Robert, 1997, 'Harmony and patriarchy: The cultural basis for Paternalistic headship among the overseas Chinese', Organisation studies;18/3;445-480

38. Yamada, Keiichi; Dec 2010; Competition In The Local Market At The Age Of Globalization: A Fraemework Of Glocalization Strategy In Fast Foods Industry; international journal of business strategy; vol. 10 issue 4, p85-98. 14p. 3 diagrams, 5 charts

39. Zegre, Sera J; Needham, Mark D; Kruger, Linda E; Rosenberger, Randall S; Oct 2012; McDonaldization and commercial outdoor recreation and tourism in Alaska; Managing Leisure, Vol. 17 Issue 4, p333-348. 16p. 1 Chart, 1 Map

40. Zimbardo G Philip, Ann L. Weber, Robert L. Johnson Allyn and Bacon, 2003 – Psychology

23

Suggested Readings

1. Heart of The Enterprise – Stafford Beer

2. Brain of The Firm – Stafford Beer

3. Societal Systems – John Warfield

4. Living Systems Theory – James Grier Miller

5. Porter E Michael. Competitive Advantage of Nations Hardcover – June 1, 1998

Printed in the United States
By Bookmasters